alt.spirit@metro.m3

Other books by Mike Riddell

Fiction
The Insatiable Moon

Non-fiction
Godzone
Threshold of the Future (forthcoming)

alt.spirit@metro.m3

MICHAEL RIDDELL

A LION PAPERBACK

Copyright © 1997 Michael Riddell

The author asserts the moral right

to be identified as the author of this work

Published by

Lion Publishing

Sandy Lane West, Oxford, England

ISBN 0 7459 3711 X

First edition 1997

10 9 8 7 6 5 4 3 2 1 0

Cover and insides designed by Gerald Rogers

A catalogue record for this book

is available from the British Library

Printed and bound in Finland

For Mark Pierson,
Brother in Arms

Introduction

The world I live in is complex. It is an urban world with noise and movement and dog turds on the footpath. I love it except for when I hate it.

Time is no longer the romantic stream of childhood in which I splashed and played. It arrives instead in chunks like segments of processed cheese.

I still haven't found what I'm looking for...

My days come at me with no time for thinking about their meaning. The phone rings, and even as I swear at it I reach to pick it up. I talk to people and can't remember what they said. I find myself looking over their shoulder for something more important, and they are doing the same.

The sky is always the same. Sure it has different pictures every day, but the screen remains the same. Stretched out like a canvas roof that someone is projecting weather on. Everyone talks about the weather, but no one talks about the sky. The basic monotony of it.

Vincent notices these things. On this day in particular, in between bites of a Big Mac, trying to hold it and eat it so that the slice of gherkin doesn't fall onto his shirt. He is sitting on a bar stool, looking at the plate-glass window which keeps him in

I graze for news. Scanning has become a way of life. Always looking for the interesting bit, the significant, the bottom line. There are voices all around me, and my energy is spent not in listening but in shutting out the ones I don't want. Sometimes I shut out my loved ones, by acci- dent. I achieve more than any of my forbears have done, but feel guilty for what I haven't done.

Often I want to escape to the past, but I'm not sure it exists. When I leave the city, I can't sleep for the quiet. And the sky is too big. There's too much milk and not enough cappuccinos.

I like to think of myself as spiritual. I am not a pointy-head bean-counter bureaucrat deadhead straight-laced politico sports-jock materialist. I want to **K N O W** the truth.

RAGE, RAGE against the dying of the

and the street out. Complaining about the piece of sky seen between the buildings.

Not that he complains out loud. Or to anyone in particular, seeing there's no one in particular who takes responsibility for the sky. The thing about relationships is having someone to complain to. Which Vincent doesn't, at this actual point in time.

Of course, there is no point in time, he is quick to remind himself. As soon as you have reached it, it has been swept away. Lost in a torrent. But in a metaphorical sort of a way, sitting on

There is no button on the remote which brings it. What's the use of technology if it can't get me the right channel?

I imagine you are different. You probably read Shirley MacLaine and overcome your cynicism. Perhaps you have learned to meditate and not swear at motorists five minutes later. Even have street maps of the astral metropolis. More likely you don't even bother about it all, just take life as it comes, let's have another cup of tea then shall we, did you see the telly last night, looks like it's going to rain, pass the Prozac would you, dearie?

I want to know what's (out) (in) there. I refuse to die before I die. There are rumours of God, and I mean to follow the trail. I wish someone could have written me a handbook, a sort of spirituality in Levi's. But no one would, so I've had to write it myself. A scrapbook of the psyche, a subway map of the heart, an entertainment guide for the cosmos. (What's on this millennium—anything interesting?)

light...

the stool while eating a Big Mac, Vincent is relatively sure that he has no relationships in the sense of **relationships**. Unless you count the cat, which you probably shouldn't.

Somewhere between school and McDonalds, I have misplaced my life. Damned careless, but there you have it. And now that it's gone, I'm not sure if I ever had one. How can you tell the difference between a life and a succession of days? Particularly if you've got nothing to compare it to. Oh well, never mind, whatever.

He picks at the shreds of lettuce in the bottom of the

There are no answers in the back of the book. Life is not a problem to be solved; it's a journey to be travelled. This is more like a cookbook written by a frustrated anorexic (gastrically challenged person). The recipes may work, or they may not. If you don't like them, write your own.

THERE IS NO PEACE; ONLY PIECES

apparently environmentally friendly cardboard box. It's hard to reconstruct a lettuce from these. He is momentarily overcome with strategies for rebuilding lettuces from the starting point of coleslaw. Or is that cabbage? Oh well, never mind, whatever.

The problem is that life is the problem, Vincent reveals to himself while using a serviette to polish his teeth. Life is not the answer but the problem. It's like one big series of lifestyle commercials, and the trick is to figure out what's being advertised. If anything at all. More likely to be a random stream of stimuli generated by a cosmic malfunction.

In the chaos there was a beginning...

But the possibility of meaning itches like a bad case of crabs. Wakes you up at night stone cold sober and staring. Trickles across the screen of consciousness on one of those days when you're trying to get your head straight after the drug of your choice. It's like a cockroach. You can't kill the bastards! You hammer away at them and they just pick themselves up and slink off to some crevice.

That's it, Vincent is smiling in the mirror column. The meaning of life is a cockroach. Which deconstructs to cock and roach. In the attempt to avoid the meaning. He checks in the

One thing I know for sure, there's
more to life than meets the **I**. And
I'm on the trail of it.

Something is happening,

And you

don't know what

it is,

do you,

Mr Jones?

mirror to see if anyone else is aware of the intergalactic
revelatory process happening in his corner of McDonalds.
They are all incognito. Plugged into their own private screens
for endless replays.

#

Marilyn is doing sex. She is concentrating on the details. It's
like you've got to imagine you were someone else watching
yourself doing sex. Like there was going to be a video replay,
and you were going to have to discuss your moves with a group

Bean Humanité

1 big bucket of mud

Shit for brains

A streak of madness

Several bars of music

1 apple (that's enough)

Hormones

The breath of God

Place ingredients in any convenient planet
(for Universe Soufflé, see earlier recipe).
Mix with bare hands until done. Divide into halves. Shape.
Leave unattended for a while. Stand well back.
Makes enough to fill several aeons.

of people. So you concentrate on getting it right, looking and sounding good.

As to the prick who's inside her **(now that was a fine move)**, he's a prop. An extra in the performance. Some John she picked up in the supermarket, of all the dumb places. If you focus on the details **(hey, quit cramping my style, you dickhead)** you can get through it alright. Get your needs met without too much damage to anyone. And then you can **(Ooooh yes)** survive.

She has options. For payment. It's just a job. You're gonna

Discovery

E=empty²

Out of it in a bare-boulder mountain
valley split by a wild stream up its
guts. With a friend. I picked up a stone
and turned it over and over. Colours
spun off the edges; it was full of magic.

Hey, look at this.

Did you ever think, he says, that
the colours might be in the rock
rather than your head?

Well, I never.

Did Isaac Newton get it wrong?
Did he even look at the apple?
Taste it? Feel the pain in his head?

sell yourself, you might as well be upfront and do it properly.
It pays better than most and you can work your own hours. I
represent the new economy. Short-term, flexible, self-employed
contract worker with an eye on quick returns. Even added a
little value to my base commodity, looking at the tattoo on her
left thigh.

After he's gone, Marilyn sits on the floor holding her
teddy bear, Patrick. He's the only safe person left in her life.
She can tell secrets to Patrick, and he keeps them to himself.
The fur is worn right through under his arm, and there's a

Those who have ears

Those who have cares

Those who have fears

Those who have tears

Let them hear... and see...

and feel... and breathe.

E=empty²

place where she can stick her finger into his insides. She does that a lot these days.

You're lucky, Patrick. You never had to grow up. You can stay the same as you always were, brown and soft. Don't you ever change, or I'll cut your arms off and shove them up your bum.

It's crap, Patrick, it's all crap. They tell you that you can be someone, make a difference, change things. So you try a few steps and fall down flat and they're all laughing. They knew all the time, you see. They've all given the game up years ago,

The world is charged with the grandeur of God.

It will flame out, like shining from shook foil;

It gathers to a greatness, like the ooze of oil

Crushed. Why do men then now not reck his rod?

Generations have trod, have trod, have trod;

And all is seared with trade; bleared, smeared with toil;

And wears man's smudge and shares man's smell: the soil

Is bare now, nor can foot feel, being shod.

but they can't bring themselves to admit it. They want to
pretend that it's different. Well, I'm not living someone else's
bullshit, Patrick. I'm sticking my face into the wind, and
taking it.

There's a weird sort of sproingy noise as Vincent pushes down
the toaster. And right at the same time he smells something. A
faint acrid burning smell. It could be the toaster's dying. But it's
not that that's got him going. It's the strange sensation on the

And for all this, nature is never spent;

   There lives the dearest freshness deep down things;

And though the last lights off the black West went

   Oh, morning, at the brown brink eastward, springs—

Because the Holy Ghost over the bent

   World broods with warm breast and with ah! bright wings.

G.M. Hopkins

---

blade of the moment **that this is awfully familiar**. A bad case of *déjà vu*, like a psychic burp. And that creeping question slicing through the early morning composure, **have I been here before?**

Well, it's undeniably true that he has been. Pushing down the toaster is hardly a novel experience. But in the larger sense, **is this evidence of reincarnation?**

It's there and then it's gone again. Like I'm watching someone watching me making my toast. As if time has fallen in on itself. But then again, so what? If I lived before, it hasn't

Earth is more like a playground than a factory. Or a laboratory. Sometimes you have to stand on your head to understand what a thin strip we occupy between earth and sky. Don't just nod your head; get out there and try it.

Discovery is not something you do. It's something that happens to you. Who discovered the Amazon? Anyone who truly saw it.

See what I mean?

The trick is to learn how to enjoy rather than interpret. It involves a lot of forgetting so that you can remember.

The universe is coded. It's not obvious. It has cool. Panache. You don't always see everything first time round. Some things take time to discover.

done me much bloody good, has it? If I lived a whole entire lifetime without figuring out what **the connections** are, then what's the point of doing it all over again? Here I am at the high point of karmic evolution, sharing a basement flat with the cat. Anyway, they never had toasters in the old days, so there goes another plan of salvation down the gurgler.

Vincent maliciously squashes an ant which chooses the wrong moment to scuttle across the bench—there's another thousand years on my account—as he grinds it under his thumb. And then feels unaccountably guilty. Picks up the cat

A man *jumps* *out of the bath and goes*

r u n n i n g down the street, shouting

'I found it! I found it!' *What is there to*

find in the bath? The soap?

Seek and you will find,

Ask and it will be given you,

Knock and the door

will be *opened...*

When we were young, we contained the entire wisdom of the universe in a simple song: Finders, keepers; losers, weepers.

and strokes it. The sun slants across the table. Where it passes through the jamjar, it refracts into rainbow colours. If you hold your hand in front, you get Technicolor fingers. But what's the point?

#

The TV is on, but not **on**, you know what I mean. Sure, Marilyn has the remote in her hand, and from time to time she fingers a button. But it's like ambient, you know? Talking head becomes skydiver becomes bonking couple becomes talking

A man went looking for the meaning of life. He passed through forests and over mountains and across seas. He talked to people along the way. All the time he was looking and listening; desperate

Only those who have received can giv

It is not always better to give than to receive. Sometimes you have to receive before you're able to give. You can only give what you've got.

for a clue to the deepest puzzle. Sometimes he thought he was onto it. He would follow up hints of mystery and words of wonder, with mounting excitement and anticipation. But always he was disappointed. The promise of meaning would dissolve like woodsmoke in the air. Many of the people he trusted turned out to be charlatans or merchants. In sadness he finally accepted that there was no meaning to life at all. The man took himself to the

head becomes car driving becomes cartoon becomes coffee commercial. Just like life. Background stuff to make you feel less alone.

On her lap is a blue chipped plate with a fragment of pizza in repose. She is picking morsels off and pushing them between her teeth. Amazing what you can do once you know how to operate on autopilot. Phrases from Psychology 101 zing across inner space, such as **autonomous nervous system**. And **retractable psyche**. What no one seems to realize is that you can do the whole life thingy in autonomous mode.

middle of a great bridge spanning a river gorge, intending to jump into oblivion. He couldn't even think of any message to leave behind. So he simply jumped.

(and vice versa)

Instead of being smashed on the rocks below, he found himself caught in a pair of arms strong enough to break his fall. 'Who are you?' asked the man of his catcher. 'I'm the one who's been looking for you,' came the reply.

So what is there left to discover in **your** life? Any room for the new? Or is it all tied down, stitched around the edges, sealed against surprise? Life has a habit of closing in on you when you're not watching.

You do things, get jobs, have relationships, eat food—and all the time you're really hiding in this cave with a candle burning. Everything is happening **out there**, beyond the cave entrance. You watch it all, but there's no connection. And people keep shouting into the cave. Come on out. We're having fun. Spend some money. Believe in yourself. Join us.

The pizza is disappearing, nibbled to death. Am I doing that? Just because I put small pieces in my mouth, does the pizza have to go? Why can't you have your pizza and eat it too? Who says? Who are they?

I still haven't found

what

I'm looking for...

At ten past three
On a wet afternoon
I observed a man
Living my life.

He carried it off
With surprising ease,
Dispensing smiles
Like painkillers

Between phone calls
He stared at the window
As if there were something dead
Fixed on the glass

'Who are you?'
I asked him.
'I have come to relieve you,'
He said.

'Don't forget my commitments,'
I tendered,
Wanting to make myself
Useful.

But the imposter
Was already busy
Signing cheques
And making appointments.

Without further ado
I turned away,
Looking for a life
That fit.

The talking head is talking to her. It is a man with a grey beard and soft eyes. He is talking about meditation. How it is good for the soul. How easy it is. Just for a moment, he looks directly into the cave. Marilyn has a sensation like the dry horrors. So incredibly tongue-cracked thirsty, and his eyes are like cold green pools. She flicks the button and he dissolves into a smiling mother changing her baby's nappy.

'There was nothing connected, no power, no water. We used to

And what shall anyone give in exchange for their life?

What woman, having ten diamonds and dropping one on the floor, doesn't go ape and start pulling the place apart looking for it? She keeps looking till she sees it twinkling in the dark. Then she gets all her friends over for a rave. She goes: 'Let's party—I found what I was looking for.'

collect buckets of water from the neighbours' outdoor tap. You had to keep a bucket by the loo to flush it. It was all a bit primitive, especially with fifteen odd of us.'

The new guy, Paul is it, looks interested only from a sense of obligation, but Vincent doesn't care. A story is a story, even if no one is really listening.

'Anyway, one of the women there was amazingly beautiful. She was Venezuelan, over here to study something or other. Only she was doing speed, spending all her money on it. Needed somewhere cheap to live, and she ended up at the

You walk past a coin on the street. There it is, shining up at you. Are you going to pick it up? No way, right? Maybe it's a trick one, glued to the ground. Somebody might be watching.

I'll leave it for some street person to pick up. Still, you never know, huh? Life may have been different if you'd stopped and bent down to check it out. Nah. Stupid.

I took a letter to my love, and on the way I dropped it... I dee, I dee, I dropped

Discovery is an attitude. Children have it when they see their first caterpillar. Sometime between then and now we lose it.

it...

There's probably a catch anyway. Hey, I'm not going to be the first one to try to pick this thing up. I've got places to go and people to see. I don't need this coin. Did I ask for it to come into my life? Damned careless people, dropping their money all over town.

squat, I don't know how. All the guys were on to her from day one, but no go. She had this sort of fiery Latin scornful stare which could make you flaccid at fifty paces.'

Paul stirs in his pool of indifference, occasionally poking his snout above the surface and snorting.

'She was totally unselfconscious. Everyone was sleeping all over the place, and she would come into the room at night, with candles burning, and strip totally naked before getting into her bed. Well the guys are all getting dry in the mouth and their right hands are disappearing nonchalantly below the

'Karin, come into my office, please.'

'What's up, Ted?'

'I'd like to know what this memo means that was on my desk this morning.'

'It doesn't mean anything except what it says.'

'I don't think we're on the same wavelength here. This memo says, '*I started feeding my mouse leftovers from my life. It liked its button pushed and would do tricks for me. Now the mouse has downloaded most of me and I am hollow and redundant. Goodbye; I'm returning to basic.*' What the hell is that supposed to mean?'

'I'm leaving, Ted. Unplugging. Logging off.
Shutting down.'

'Are you all right, Karin?'

'Are you all right, Ted?'

---

blankets. And the women all think she's such a bitch because she's so drop-dead beautiful. Estiva, that was her name.

'One day this cop turns up with all the usual rant and tells us we're going to be kicked out, he's got the court order etc etc. We're all pretty ratted off, cause we like the place, but we're sort of resigned to it, you know? A squat is only ever good for so long. But Estiva, she suddenly tells this cop that we have permission to be there. And she's got the papers to prove it. We're like, huh?

'So she takes the cop into the bedroom to show him these

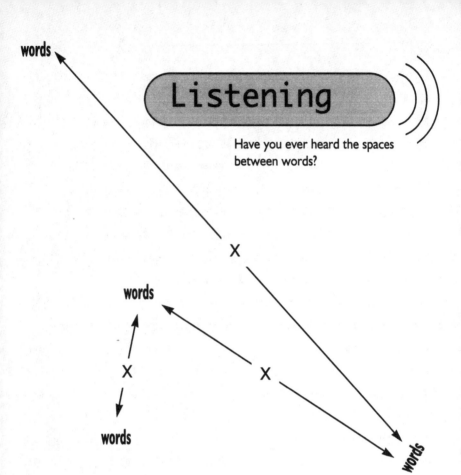

Listening

Have you ever heard the spaces between words?

papers, and shuts the door. Twenty minutes later he comes out with his legs buckling under him, and says she's right, we have permission to stay. We're all totally blown away by this, the ice virgin turning it up for the sake of our future. But even though we have some drinks to celebrate, and tease her all night, Estiva's saying nothing.

'Next morning, she's gone. All her stuff is gone, there's no note, nothing. That was the last time any of us ever saw her. We stayed on for another three months before they finally kicked us out. We used to spend hours talking about her, trying to

In the beginning was the

WORD...

... in the end there were only

words.

Listening does not come naturally. The city is pumping with sound; noise coming at you like a street gang. Words fighting for the main chance, the big hit, the hard sell. Is there a space on the planet where cellphones don't ring? Strings of syllables sparking across the synapses; constant consonants vaulting vowels; tight trendy tautologies numbing the neurons. They're storming every orifice.

figure her out. But we never could. I still wonder about her from time to time. Why would she do that for us, and then leave? What was in it for her?'

'Beats me,' says Paul. 'Another drink?'

#

Marilyn's apartment is on the third floor. She likes to call it an apartment, even though it's really only a flat. It has a view over two rooftops before the brick wall puts a dead end to the horizon. There is a nest on the nearest roof which she likes to

Cynthia wanted some peace. She boarded up all her windows. Lined her walls with egg cartons. She blocked the chimney and ripped the phone off the wall. It didn't work. The bass from her neighbour's stereo snuck up through the foundations. A helicopter chopped her quiet into coleslaw. Cynthia upped the ante. She inserted earplugs and covered them with earmuffs. Then she climbed onto her bed and put a pillow over her head. Only then did she become aware of the noise coming from the inside...

NOISE NOISE NOISE NOISE NOISE NOIS NOISE NOISE NOISE NOISE

---

watch. The baby birds getting fed. All the work that the parent bird does (is it a male or a female—who the hell knows?) collecting food all day long. And putting it into the babies' mouths. Where does that come from?

Next door is Mr Bateup. A grizzly old codger who bangs on the wall when the stereo is on, but has his TV going all day at 80 decibels. He opens his front door a crack whenever he hears Marilyn coming. 'I know what you're doing in there,' he muttered to her in the hall one day as she was guiding a nervous customer up the stairs. 'Piss off,' was all she could

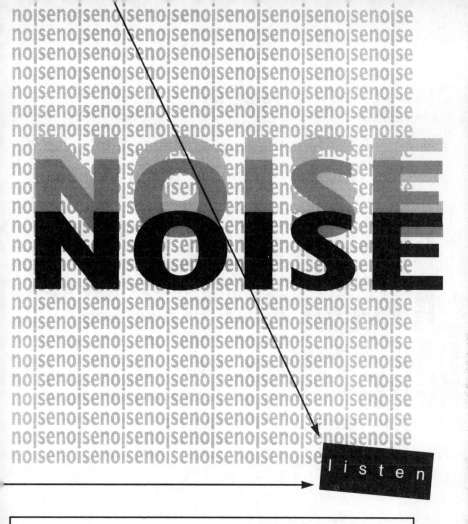

NOISE
NOISE

listen

manage in response. Later she thought of all sorts of clever replies she could have used. Story of her life.

On top of the bedside cabinet she has some crystals. Her friend Paula with the legs had told her all about crystals, and their amazing powers. What they could do for you in terms of acting like **receivers** for positive energy. You know, like they used to have these things called crystal radios, because crystals just **collect** stuff out of the air. Marilyn was really excited when she bought them. Apart from anything else, they were good to look at and hold.

q u i e t [kwl-et] n.

silence,
hush,
calm,
serenity,
solitude,
retreat,
peace,
tranquillity,
repose.

An old man used to sit for hours on end in church. One day a priest asked him what God talked to him about.

'God doesn't talk; God just listens,' was his reply.

'Well then, what do you talk to God about?'

'I don't talk either. I just listen.'

When she got home, she followed Paula's instructions for **placing them in the right pattern**. You had to close your eyes and move them without thinking about them, until you started to get positive vibes. Marilyn got a violent attack of hiccups, and it was hard to concentrate on her inner world. Am I feeling better now? Or like this? In the end she got tired and left them where they were, and they sort of stayed there. Except for when they got bumped, which didn't seem to make any noticeable difference.

You never know, though. Like, I'm certain there is some

NOISE

quiet

There is no escape from noise. Quiet lies in the midst of it. You have to enter the pool in order to find it.

The towers are telling of God;
the asphalt is humming the rhythm of Life.
Every cappuccino morning is a message;
each neon night a sign in the sky.
There is no speech, nor are there words;
their sound is silence;
Yet their voice is heard in every city,
and their lyrics speak in every street.

sort of **power** around that we can tap into. There's just too much unexplained stuff. All those UFOs that the government creeps know about, but keep covering up in case people find out what's really going on. And Nostradamus and all that— it's just too obvious that there is **something** out there. But how do you get a handle on it? Because even Paula, who seems to know so much about this shit, is still pretty screwed up. How spiritually aware can you be when you're on the game?

Marilyn watches the mother bird (she's decided it must be a mother) swoop in with the latest packet of takeaways. The

Words are a form of communication; they are full of meanings. Some are more important than others. Occasionally I squeeze a bit of myself in the stratosphere. You may ignore it altogether, not even recognize that anything's happening. You might receive it like a tennis ball, returning

---

Listanga

1 pair ears (reamed)
Stuffing to keep them apart
3 measures silence
Several glasses wine (optional)
A single focus
Basting of Time

Fold ingredients together gently.
Leave to stand (or sit). Baste frequently. Avoid sudden movement or noise, as this may cause dish to deflate.
A little goes a long way.

---

into the case of a word, which never quite contains it. And then I throw it out there, hoping you might notice. It's a risky business, having a poorly clothed bit of yourself floating around the serve from a tight grid of strings. You may grab the case, empty it on the floor, and fill it with your own stuff. Then I will remain in my loneliness.

---

baby birds opening their mouths and going ape in anticipation. Sitting there waiting to be fed. It must be nice to have a mother.

#

'So tell me, Paul, what are you passionate about?'

'What d'you mean?'

'What turns you on in life? What are you excited about? What would you die for?' Vincent is doing well with that delicious alcoholic glow making everything loose.

On the other hand, perhaps you will open it, and carefully unfold the contents in an attempt to understand them. That's okay; it was intended as a gift. When you receive my gift, you receive me. A bridge is built between us. But if you are not listening, we will pass each other by.

Perhaps reality is very similar. Among the words there may be the odd special one, planted among us like a seed.

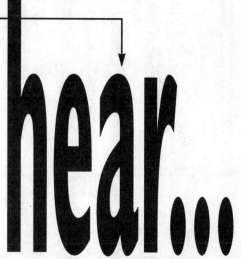

Those who have ears, let them hear...

'Well, I dunno. I play football on the weekends, if that's what you mean.'

'No, look, I'm not talking about hobbies. I mean you and I, we both work in the same branch of the bank, right? We punch numbers and little green squiggly things come up on the screens and we pass bits of paper back and forwards. We live in places that we go home to at the end of every day. We have weekends where we do things that we want to do. We sometimes go to the pub or to the movies or to a football game or to a gig. But what's it all about? Is that what we're born for?

This is the word of the Lord

Listen! Do you want to know a secret? [Or should it be the other way round?]

Someone is speaking amidst the noise, but the static makes it hard to hear. A certain amount of time must be spent in tuning the station.

Is it worth living for? That's what I want to know.

'Take it easy, Vince. We all have bad days once in a while. No point in getting all morbid about it.'

'Morbid? I'll tell you what's morbid, Phil.'

'Paul.'

'What?'

'It's Paul. You said Phil.'

'Yeah, right, whatever.' Vincent is taking another slug of beer, which is improving in quality by the mouthful. 'Morbid,'

The Joy of

Aural Sex

Begin by disrobing the ears. Take off the filters and invite all the sounds in your small sector of the universe to come in.

Identify the sounds one by one. The cars rushing past, the neighbours arguing, **2** *the sirens, kids yelling, dogs barking, teenagers raving.*

As you recognize each one, savour it for a short time before depositing it in a round tin with a lid on. ← **3**

4 → *Now hear the chatter on the inside. Identify the voices, listen to them, bin them.*

Be still. ← **5**

6 → *Still.*

Note: This may take a year or two to get right, give or take. But no risk of AIDS!

(Even hearing aids)

---

wiping the froth from his lips, 'is living this useless life without asking any questions about it. Morbid is to treat a job in the bank as normal, like it was what we were supposed to be doing with life. Morbid is going through the motions day after day until the funeral director turns up to take you away in a big black car. You ever think about death, Phil? Ever think about the big full stop? When your heart stops beating and there's no blood going to your brain any more, and suddenly you're just a big misshapen lump of meat? They take you away and they put you in a bloody freezer, for God's sake, because you're just a lump of meat and you might go off and stink the place up.'

Sweeper Hears God On High

Samuel Budge, street-sweeper of Clapham Junction,

today claimed to have been the recipient of a divine communication.

Mr Budge, who has no formal theological qualifications,

insisted that he had received a genuine revelation.

'I was just making my way down the High Street, minding my own business,

when I saw a bloke playing guitar and singing,' said Mr Budge.

He stopped and listened for a time, while checking the immediate vicinity for litter.

'While I was listening, I came over all funny, and that's when I heard it,' he said.

Mr Budge was reluctant to describe exactly what it was he had heard,

except to say that life would never be the same for him again.

'It was wonderful,' he recounted, 'right marvellous. In fact, it was too marvellous for...'

Mr Budge was accompanied by a police officer to the local Community Mental

Health clinic. No further action is to be taken.

'I think you might have had enough. I'd better be going anyway.'

'Had enough? You're right, I've had enough. You just go and catch a bus and leave me here, because you're right. I've had enough. In fact, I may even have had too much.'

#

I had a mother of sorts. I remember her crying in the bedroom, mostly. Big purply-black bruises which would go yellow as the swelling went down. The thumping and the

Risk

sort of event. It can start early. It's the small choices, in the end, that determine whether we will live or not. To protect or to discover, to conserve or to create, to sleep or to dance. Risk-taking is a strategy for living. It can become as much of a habit as its opposite. Some people take risks because they're stupid. They can't see the danger. But others see the danger and consciously choose to accept it for the sake of freedom. The thing about bungee-jumping is, you don't know if the bungee is attached until you reach the end. Life is much the same.

Basic rule of thumb: anything worthwhile is dangerous. Life hurts, and the alternative is death. There's always a time when shutting down seems more attractive than exposing yourself to more pain. Dying isn't a once-for-all

BEWARE
of Security Chains

screaming in the night. She had beautiful long black hair. I would play with it for hours, stroking it and plaiting it. I remember the feel of it through my fingers. She used to hide money in a shoe, and sometimes she would buy me something—an ice-cream or a dress from the charity shop.

She would come and clean me up after he'd been at me. Take me into the bathroom, with soap and water and a towel. She was gentle, careful not to rub hard where it was already sore. Often times there would be these silent tears running down her cheeks and she would hold me and I'd say, 'It's

In the end you can only keep what you're prepared to lose. The older you get, the more tempting it is to start putting defences in place.

It brings **D E A T H**. The world may be ruled by the anally retentive, but it is those of a looser physiology who throw the best parties.

What you need is not security, but the verve of the gambler; not a firm place to stand, but the style of the swimmer.

Building protective walls to keep the sea out. Covering all the possibilities so that you can keep life under **CONTROL**. But to eliminate all danger is to eliminate all possibility. The absence of risk does not bring contentment.

What good is it to control everything, and lose your own soul?

alright, Mummy.' And then in the morning we never talked about it, and it was like either a secret or a dream. He would be sitting there eating his breakfast, like nothing had happened.

There was a day we went on a picnic. It was the sunniest day ever, and we caught the train, the three of us. He was smiling and joking, the only day I ever saw him like that. We walked from the station to this huge park, with trees and grass. There was a blanket, and food—even a cake with raisins in it. The sky was blue and I was doing handstands all over the place.

Caution should be used cautiously, abandonment with abandon.

In deep intimate love we almost lose ourselves. Sexual encounter has the disturbing effect of making your boundaries go wobbly. For a short space of time the I-thou thing falls apart, and both of you are laid totally bare and vulnerable. At the same time you may be risking conception, AIDS, and any number of STDs. So what the hell is **safe sex**?

Let's face it...

is in your face, the road is at your feet, your hair streams out behind you, you are a very small distance away from total annihilation. In a car you sit in a comfortable seat, the windscreen protects you from the wind, there is a stereo to play your favourite music, you may even have air conditioning to adjust the temperature. It's so good that you hardly even know you're travelling. But wait a minute; isn't the point to be travelling? It's this concern for **safety** which is the evidence that I am growing older.

Life is not safe.

I find myself trying to protect more and risk less. I travel in a car instead of riding a motorbike. Have you ever thought about it? On a bike the wind

I went off looking for squirrels in a patch of bush. I liked being on my own.

He came to look for me. I saw him looking at me and I knew the day was over. She came and found us when he was still on top of me. She picked up a branch and started hitting him, and he punched her. I just watched, and pulled my knickers up. He was worried people would come because of the noise she was making, crying and shouting.

No day has ever been as sunny as that one started out to be.

There is an inner world and an outer world. On the inside is me, and on the outside is not-me. But where are the boundaries? How tight are they? This question of personal boundaries has something to do with the willingness to risk.

Latex may be impermeable: But it ain't pretty.

Chance your arm

#

The only legacy from her mother was this silver crucifix. She didn't even know she had died until two weeks after it had happened. By then it was too late. The funeral was over, and it wasn't as if there was a grave to go and visit. No one had requested any ashes. There was nothing left except the crucifix, which her auntie had kept for her. 'Your mother gave it to me and said she wanted you to have it.'

It represented some sort of vague Catholic roots, Marilyn

Partying

At regular intervals, it is necessary to party. Who knows why? It's one of those things that you just don't question. To survive is animal; to party is human; to be a party animal is to be divinely human.

I'll tell you the truth. I can't quite cope with life. If I try to tough it out on my own, it doesn't work. I find I have to get together with some other people and get my rocks off. I need reminding what it feels like to be **alive**. The capacity to party is a greatly undervalued quality in today's market. The great test of a

If you don't move your feet to the music, you won't understand the lyrics...

supposed. She could recall being taken along to Mass a couple of times. It was like visiting some other planet, with men wearing dresses and pronouncing strange spells. Drab people sitting and kneeling and standing to some secret signals that Marilyn could never seem to pick up. The long queue up the aisle to get some sort of serious-looking medicine from the front. What connection it had with anything else in the whole of the world she never quite understood. It was pleasant enough to be somewhere with her mother alone.

The crucifix had been stuck away in a drawer until

spiritual leader is, would you want to party with this person?
Well, would you?

Party Party Party STOP (don't)

Party Party

You don't have to get out of it in order to party. Most times it's better to get into it instead. Who says pain and partying don't go together?

Madonna started wearing one and it became fashionable. Then she had dug it out and looked at it properly for the first time. It was quite heavy and solid. It looked great, particularly with a low-cut top. There was a man pinned to the cross, like a butterfly. Best place for him, she thought. She liked to wear it, although one John had made her cover it up and hide it before they started.

Perhaps he felt threatened by the competition.

#

It's my party and I'll
CRY if I want to...

From time to time the psychic pressure builds to danger level. You and I, we owe it to each other not to incubate our toxic stuff. Let's be serious about our responsibility to party.

Life was meant to be lived in its extremes. It's not the sort of thing you can eat the middle out of. All or nothing, and partying is a way of exploring the edges.

The old man was crippled and in a wheelchair. One day he went to a wedding. He talked to the bride and groom, telling them of his own wedding. He spoke of the music that had been played, the dancing that had been done. As he spoke, he began to hum one of the old tunes. He got louder and louder, and his foot began to tap to the music. Others joined in, and he burst into song. Then before he knew what he was doing, he was out of the wheelchair and dancing before all the guests, to show them how the steps had gone. And all those years leading up to that day, he thought he had forgotten the tune.

For a moment the two worlds merge, and he is uncertain which one is his home. Then his bedroom begins to get the upper hand, and with the benefit of consciousness he recognizes: I have had a dream. It lingers like someone looking over his shoulder. As the mental paralysis begins to subside, the images come as memories, this time with enough distance to be pondered.

He was in a house. It was an old house, knocked around but comfortable. He was sitting in a comfortable chair, looking out the window. It was a large window, and outside he could see

same
safe
sage
sane
save
rave
rage

God loves to party

people passing by. He could see out, but they couldn't see in. Many of them were carrying large packages on their backs, and they were wearied and weighed down by them. The people were trudging along, their eyes on the ground in front of them.

Vincent wondered where they were all going. They seemed to be headed in the same direction, but without much interest in what they were doing. He went up to the window to watch them more closely. 'Where are you all going?' he shouted. But no one could hear him. They just kept shuffling along, one after the other. While he was watching, he gradually

Dreaming

What is a dream? Is it a chemical thing caused by pigging out on the cheeseboard before sleep? Is it an astral thing? And where do they come from, these B-grade movies of the interior? What dyslexic editor is working on this stuff?

You know that moment just as you're waking up? And the dreamworld is about equal with the other stuff? So which is reality? How can you tell? What would happen if one day you woke up from life?

I had a dream. I was on this island in the middle of the ocean. I felt so terribly alone. I lay there in my loneliness, calling out to God. There was no response. Then there was a terrible shaking and moving, and I was afraid. To my amazement, the island began to rise into the sky. As I looked down I realized that what I had been lying on was not an island at all, but a giant hand. And I was being held safely in the palm of that hand, and being lifted gently into the presence of God. But after all, it was only a dream.

---

became aware of a weight on his own back. And then it dawned on him; he was carrying a package as well.

He became aware of a distant noise. It was a persistent knocking. He tried to ignore it, but it forced itself on him. Persistent, demanding knocking. Turning around to locate the source of it, he recognized that it was someone at the door, wanting to come in. Vincent went to open the door, and then suddenly became scared. 'Who's there?' he called. 'You know,' was the answer. And he did know, of course. He recognized the voice, even though he still couldn't picture who it belonged to.

The old ones will see visions,
And the young ones dream
dreams

Ever consider that dreams might be a language? A language which uses pictures instead of words. Which is not such a bad thing, if you're like me and suffocating in words. Perhaps dreams are the language of the heart, the language of the psyche, the language of the spirit. But who understands that language any more?

And if dreams are a language, who or what is speaking?

The cold hard facts have a habit of leading me astray. I have learnt to value the warm soft dream which gives understanding. Dreams are one of the ways in which new things come

Dream On.

He opened the door, and there was Estiva, in peasant dress and all her beauty. 'What have you asked her. Her eyes were so lovely and peaceful take this,' she said, and suddenly she was holding the package, and Vincent was feeling refreshed and strong. 'Does it belong to you?' he said. 'Not really, but I'm happy to take it for you.' Then she reached over and ever so gently brushed his lips with her own, and he must have woken. He lay there for some time, reluctant to diminish the almost physical sensation of her lips on his. Wondering, what is the meaning of all this?

into existence. They are part of the giftedness of life. How many times has someone woken with a new idea, a new tune, a new solution? There is more to our lives than what is on the surface. With the number of filters we have operating to save us from dweebs, it may only be in the vulnerability of sleep that we are receptive to the inner world.

Where do our dreams go when we're awake? Do they carry on happening without us? Is it us who leaves or them?

There was a time when all the important leaders in the world had a council of people whose main task was to interpret dreams. It is possible that they were primitive and superstitious, that they didn't have the courage to act.

Quick Quiz:

Did Martin Luther King have a dream, or did a dream have Martin Luther King?

● ● ● ● ● ● ● ● ● ● ● ● ● ● ● ● ● ●

#

The latté leaves a frothy mark on Paula's upper lip, which she quickly wipes away with the serviette.

'You're a bit sad today, Marilyn love. A little bit of aural sag, I can see there. Of course it's not a good week for you, with Saturn doing its little thing at the moment. You want to stay indoors as much as you can.'

On the other hand, it is possible that they were simply paying attention to all the sources of information available.

And then at odd moments, the disturbing thought will come to me:

'It was you that asked me out for a coffee. I was happy watching the box.'

'Yes, well of course you've got to make exceptions for certain people who are spiritually invigorating, who put energy back in rather than draining it all out. God knows you look like you could use a bit of a psychic booster shot.'

'Why can't you get it in some sort of medicinal form, like HRT? Just go down to the doctor for a spiritual transfusion—it'd save a lot of time.'

Cynicism

Did you know that gullible isn't actually spelt like that? Did you

Why is everyone so down on cynics? The city I live in eats the gullible for breakfast. Being cynical isn't a sign of pessimism—it's a survival technique. In a world where everyone is trying to sell you something, cynicism is a prophylactic (go look it up). You have to keep your eyes open. If you can't distinguish an urban myth from a metanarrative, then you'll be destined to suckerhood for the rest of your metro life.

Anyone who's really interested in what's going down in life has to be a tad cynical. I like to reserve the right to evaluate truth for myself. Cynicism is a useful tool for distinguishing the naive from the naff from the nasty.

'Aren't we the little cynic today? But honestly, Marilyn, I've been reading this book which is an absolute **must** for you. It's all about planetary forces and the alignment of geomagnetic fields.' She pauses for a long pull at the latté, with astonished eyes over the top of the cup.

'Well, go on. I know you're going to tell me about it anyway.'

'Now the man who wrote it used to be a scientist with NASA, and they sacked him because he knew too much about the encounter with aliens and was threatening to talk about it.

It's a technique for dealing with the depressing reality of life while not becoming a part of it. Cynics are often criticized for standing outside the system. Like, you want us to become part of the **system**?

The whole point of cynicism is to try to protect what's on the inside, by making a little shelter. It can have unwelcome side effects. Exploring the inner world calls for faith, trust, vulnerability. Cynicism has a habit of invading the wrong space.

So I find myself trying to be a hard-nosed no-nonsense tough-minded spiritual pilgrim. I hope to find meaning while kicking holes in the meanings suggested by others. It's a tough act.

Sinner

→

Schism

Anyway, he went into hiding in the desert for five years, and one day when he was writing his journal, he discovered all this **amazing** stuff coming out on his page. He realized that he was being used to dictate a book, and so he wrote it all down and now it's been published.'

'I don't think this coffee's as good as it used to be when Jackie was here. Sorry, go on.'

'It turns out that there's this secret pattern of cosmic forces built into the earth's crust, that was established thousands of years ago when Earth used to be a base for galactic travellers.

The optimist believes we live in the best of all possible worlds. The pessimist fears this is true.

But one thing I refuse. I will not become a credulous quiche-eating cretin who believes six impossible things before breakfast.

Is there no hope for cynics? Are we destined always to rip the plant of faith out of the ground to check if it's really growing? Is it possible to live in the real world and still be interested in what the spock is happening? Don't give up on truth too easily.

She believed in nothing: only her scepticism kept her from being an atheist.

JEAN-PAUL SARTRE

The information was passed on to certain trusted people, and that's what all the pyramids and Stonehenge and stuff are about.'

'What d'you mean?'

'They're markers, to show where the main currents flow. This book has big charts which show where all the forcefields exist right across the earth.'

'So what's the point of it?'

'Well, darling, it's simple. What you need to do is work

Test everything, including yourself.
Anything or anyone who can't handle
the questions probably wasn't worth
it in the first place.

He said to them,

'Unless I see the nail holes in his hands, and put my finger in them and my hand in his side, I will not believe.'

out where your nearest transcontinental magnetic node is, and point your bed with your feet facing in that direction. I've already done it, and I wake up every morning feeling just so fantastically alive, glowing all over. While you're asleep, you see, all the psychic energy just seeps into you.'

'So where's the nearest node to here?'

'I've worked it all out, using the charts, and it's in the direction of the old gasworks. You just aim the foot of your bed at the old gasometer, and it'll do wonders for you.'

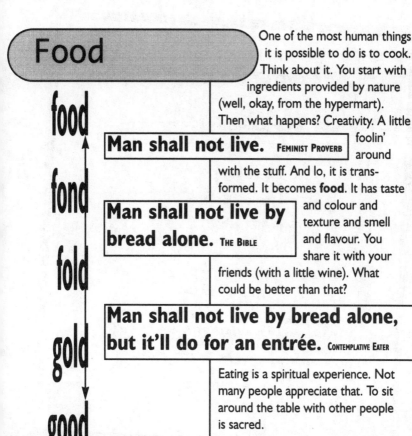

Food

food
fond
fold
gold
good

One of the most human things it is possible to do is to cook. Think about it. You start with ingredients provided by nature (well, okay, from the hypermart). Then what happens? Creativity. A little foolin' around with the stuff. And lo, it is transformed. It becomes **food**. It has taste and colour and texture and smell and flavour. You share it with your friends (with a little wine). What could be better than that?

Man shall not live. FEMINIST PROVERB

Man shall not live by bread alone. THE BIBLE

Man shall not live by bread alone, but it'll do for an entrée. CONTEMPLATIVE EATER

Eating is a spiritual experience. Not many people appreciate that. To sit around the table with other people is sacred.

'But that'd mean I'd have to have my bed diagonally across the room!'

'When it comes to your spiritual well-being, Marilyn, I've told you before—there's no room for compromises. You've got to use everything you can find to get a leg up that spiritual ladder.'

'I think I'll have another piece of fruitcake. You want any?'

It's a very mellow stone. Just enough to intensify everything, without the paranoia. Sitting on a park bench, Vincent is

Divine Consommé

4 or 5 friends (tenderized)

I large table

Large measure of time

Liberal lacing of laughter

Several bottles of marinade for all

I ounce of honest confrontation

I serious cook

Food without end

*Pay particular attention to ensuring that the work area
is free from condemnation. Apply friends to table, mixing carefully.
Blend in time, laughter, marinade and confrontation, gently,
to avoid the mix falling flat. Finally add cook and food.
It may be necessary to apply moderate force to separate
friends from table.*

watching the dusk rinse the colour out of the landscape. There is a wonderful stillness, despite the fact that rush-hour traffic is grunting and sighing its way up the hill. The leaves just hang there, breathing. And the air is so sweet you gain some pleasure from every lungful. Above the trees the sky is turning negligée pink. Dark silhouettes of birds slice and dive. There is a duck calling somewhere.

He sees the man coming. A rather stooped man with balding head. There is a gentleness and carefulness in the way he is walking, as if each step were considered. The man pauses

The single most important thing you can do to develop your spirituality is to eat and drink with others. If it should happen that you can get some strangers around the table, so much the better. Food enables talk—it is the visible sign of love. But remember to take time:

Fast food is bad for you.

at the bench, smiles at Vincent, and asks the question with his eyes. Vincent is expansive, happy to share his space and his evening.

'It's a beautiful evening,' Vincent offers.

'Yes. Each time has its beauty, but there is a serenity at the dying of the day which is very satisfying.'

The way the man speaks is different. As if he were at the centre of a great calm, and the words were drifting outwards like twigs in a pond.

The first miracle of Jesus was to turn untold gallons of water into wine. After that the crowds didn't need any more miracles. Until they got hungry. Then he took two fish, five loaves, and a little recipe which he got from his father, and cooked up a storm. Eventually it became necessary to put a stop to him. They said:

You are a glutton and a winebibber.

He commended them for their powers of observation and discernment. 'The food I eat you have never tasted,' he said.

I like to cook because I like to eat. I like to cook for others because I like to bring joy into their lives. I like the sizzle and splatter, the stirring and straining, the peeling and pounding, the steam and smell, the patience and panic, the slicing and searing, the placing and preening, the sipping and serving. I like to create magical things out of very little.

I like to eat because I like food. I like to share food and appreciation of it with other people. I like the colour and contrast, the savouring and sucking, the chewing and crunching, the tasting and

The first ingredient is always

'I find it easy to relax in a place like this,' Vincent adds.

'It is good to be able to relax wherever you are.'

'That's a bit difficult where I work—it's all hustle and bustle, everyone in a hurry.

'Forgive me, but is it not true that relaxation comes from the inside rather than from the outside?'

'Maybe, but there's nothing too relaxed about my inside. The reason I come to places like this is to try to get some peace.'

talking, the shape and style, the spice
and sweetness, the relishing and
remembering. I like the long slow
digesting of all that is good.

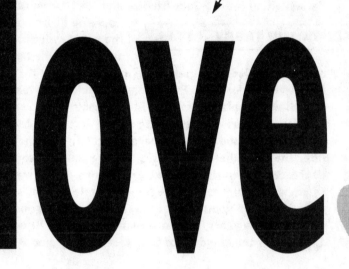

love

'I don't wish to be rude, but I wonder what it is that causes you to be disturbed?'

'Good question—I wish I knew. It's all pretty heavy stuff— the meaning of life, my place in the scheme of things, which tin of catfood to open next.'

'These are serious questions for a young man to be asking. Where are you looking for the answers?'

'Nowhere at the moment. I can't seem to find anyone who even understands what I'm asking, let alone getting any help with answers.'

Hunger is a way of life.

In a far-off land there lived a man who was very religious. He lived an austere life and was determined to remain pure until the coming of the kingdom of God. Through many hardships he endured. But the day came when his patience ran out. 'The kingdom will never come,' he said to himself. 'I may as well make the most of what I've got.' So he withdrew an enormous amount of money from his savings, and decided to throw a dinner party. He invited all his religious friends, and then for good measure he invited a lot of the people who lived nearby; people he had

Food comes in many forms.

always regarded as sinners. The preparations for the feast went on for days. Eventually everything was ready and all the people assembled. The righteous were very concerned about who they were sitting next to. But gradually the food and wine began to soften their hearts. After the meal there was music, and the sinners began to dance. Soon even the devout were dancing. There was a wonderful atmosphere of laughter and celebration, and everyone had a good time. 'I haven't had such a good time for many years,' said one man to the host. 'It was almost as if the kingdom of God were already among us.'

'Do you help your cat to eat?'

'I beg your pardon?'

'Do you help your cat to eat?'

'I'm not sure what you're getting at, but no, I don't help my cat to eat. Apart from opening the can and putting the food where the cat can get at it.'

'Nobody can help you find the answers, apart from helping you see in which direction to look.'

'Where have you found help in answering the questions?'

Resistance

How do you remember who you are in this world? Am I the person I see reflected in shop windows? Is that me who puts on different images for different gigs? Or the fool that my friends know me as? What about the sociopathic character on the inside of my skull? Is that me?

Conformity seems to be running at around 15 atmospheres. I find it hard to breathe under that sort of pressure. But if I don't stay true to myself, if I don't hang on to the vital core of being, then what have I got left?

zero

'I follow the way of the Buddha. But my answers may not be the ones to answer your questions. You must be like your cat, and keep your nose to the air. Good luck.'

With that the man was gone, fading into the gathering gloom more suddenly than he had appeared. Vincent continued sitting there as night fell.

It's not the first time she's thought about it. Once before she bought a length of stout cord from the hardware shop. But

Just because

I have to find strategies for resisting the mind-numbing, bland-branding, shoe-shining sock-crushers, who want to make me like them. The bureaunazis of the soul. Watch out for them.

I'm paranoid,

Subversion is a form of resistance. It's a game to be played from the inside. Once you know who you are it becomes easy. You need to have some-where to stand which is outside the system; some source of life which is inaccessible to the technotyrants.

it doesn't mean

Resistance starts in your own heart. It's so easy to get passive: to fall asleep in front of the telly and wake up to find that you mortgaged your soul. Life doesn't happen without putting up some sort of a fight. Keep the faith, sisters and brothers, keep the faith.

people aren't

watching me.

then she read that death by hanging could take as much as fifteen minutes. She couldn't face the prospect of hanging there twitching. It had to be either sudden or gentle.

Which is why Marilyn is contemplating the bottle of sleeping tablets.

She takes the top off and pours them into her palm. Then she pours them back again. It's the unknown quality about death that makes it so hard. If you could be sure that there was nothing but oblivion, the leap into the dark, the eternal sleep, it would all be easy. But there is that haunting doubt: what if?

Power follows the path of least resistance.

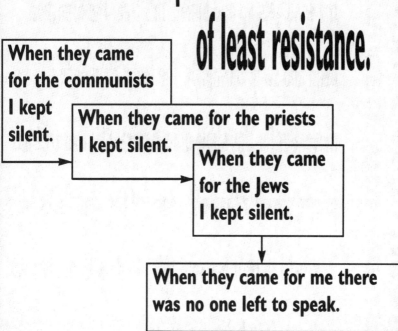

When they came for the communists I kept silent.

When they came for the priests I kept silent.

When they came for the Jews I kept silent.

When they came for me there was no one left to speak.

The prospect of further pain is intolerable, when all you are calling out for is numbness.

The cave is deep and dark. It is a comfortable place for her to be, far away from other people and their demands. There is a faint light at the entrance, but very faint. Marilyn can feel the walls pressing in. She does not resist, but sits there in a form of practised passivity. She holds the pill bottle in one hand. With the other she unthinkingly fingers the cross around her neck, rubbing her thumb up and down the surface of it.

THE TROUBLE WITH NORMAL IS IT ALWAYS GETS WORSE

BRUCE COCKBURN

Outside my window there is a huge tree. Now and again the wind gets up and buffets this tree. The branches bend and sway alarmingly. The trunk even begins to move. But for the whole of its natural life, that tree has proved stronger than any efforts of the wind to dislodge it. Why? I think it has something to do with the bits you can't see, deep below the surface.

Is there anything out there? One last chance, she decides. One absolutely final fling at this thing, and then that's it. If there's anyone listening, you better know I'm serious. Say something, before I can hear nothing. The silence is complete. She tightens the lid on the bottle, with regret.

Vincent reads *Jonathan Livingstone Seagull* for the third time. It is inspiring, majestic, and all so easy. Beside his bed there is the evidence of the last month's investigation into Buddhism. Also a

Some tips on developing resistance.

1. Don't wear a watch. That way you won't have time on your hands.

2. Every now and again light your fire with a significant piece of paper money. Alternatively wipe your bottom with it (care required here).

Nole Illegitimi Carborundum

3. Play computer games (or their equivalent) at work without trying to hide what you're doing.

4. Practise random acts of umpremeditated stupidity.

5. Refuse to believe in the reality of macroeconomics, and do not bow to the altar of the free market.

6. Never accept any explanation for why things can't be done that way.

Stay Staunch!

tinfoil packet, a pouch of rolling tobacco and an empty tequila bottle. The trail of a dissolute disciple. He is finding the idea of Buddhism enormously attractive. Apart from some continuing scepticism about reincarnation.

But the practice of it, that's what is tearing him apart. The eight-fold path is good—I'd recommend it to anyone. Anyone but me. The absence of drugs has got me stuffed for a start. It's not like I don't try: it's like the whole thing is more suited to monks who can wander round in robes than bank clerks who like to unwind after work.

belonging somewhere can I make sense of who I am. Over the years I have come to value the shaping power of community.

The need to stand alone. The need to belong. How do you hold them together? I have tried to get by on my own, to be a rugged individual. Apart from the fact that I lack ruggedness, it doesn't work anyway. Sure I need my spaces; but without people around they don't seem like spaces—more like a vacuum.

At last I have had to face up to it: I need people. I need relationships. Only in the context of

All the lonely people; where do they all come from?

He tried meditating. Twice he fell asleep, most times he ended up thinking about problems at work like how to account for the $57.00 they were out at the end of day. The very last episode of applied contemplation, he felt he was getting somewhere. Until the cat stalked him from behind, pounced on his feet and bit his toes. Vincent did not imagine the ensuing string of invective did much for his own or the cat's spiritual state.

He is aware that it's his own problem—that he doesn't have enough discipline. But he doesn't know how to go about getting discipline. From what he's read so far, discipline is

I'm not sure any more that it's possible to be human apart from community. All of us need a place to stand—a group of people who know us as we really are and yet still love us. A community is a place where you can fight without fear of rejection.

The search for truth is not a solo venture. We need to hear all the voices if we are going to make sense out of the universe.

Reality is not some abstract luge which everyone has to ride. It is more like a garden for walking through.

Let a thousand opinions bloom

gained by being disciplined, which is a fairly circular argument. And he's not big in the patience department either. I want enlightenment, and I want it now. In the background, a piece of inspired programming has U2 singing 'But I still haven't found what I'm looking for...' Vincent throws the book across the room and heads out the door to the pub.

#

How it happened, whether accidentally or with some sort of **purpose** (Paula would have no doubt), Marilyn could never say.

There was once an old monastery which had lost its inspiration. The same routines were performed as they always had been, but there were no new novices and little enthusiasm for the rites of prayer.

The abbot saw all this and grieved. At a loss as to how to change things, he paid a visit to an old hermit who lived in the woods. The hermit welcomed him and spread the table with bread and cheese and wine. After they had eaten together, the recluse addressed the abbot.

'You and your brothers have lost the fire of God. You come seeking wisdom from me. I will tell you a secret, but you can only repeat it once. After that no one must say it aloud again.' The hermit then looked deep into the eyes of the abbot and said, 'The Messiah is among you.'

They were both silent as the abbot considered the import of this saying. 'Now you must leave,' the hermit said.

Returning to the monastery, the abbot called all the monks together and told them that he had a teaching which had been given by God. He added that the teaching was never to be repeated out loud again. Then the abbot looked at each of his brothers, and said, 'The hermit says that one of us is the Messiah.'

The monks were startled. 'What could it mean?' they wondered silently. 'Is John with

Community

The mechanics were simple enough. There was a knock at her door, and when she opened it there was a courier package outside. No name on it, but it was her address on the label. She took it inside, with all the excitement that goes with an unopened parcel.

She took her time opening it. Marilyn understood delayed gratification, particularly since it was the one thing most of her clients were incapable of. When the bubblewrap and the last layer of tissue came off, there was a bottle of expensive perfume and two tickets to a rock concert. She went back through the

the big nose the Messiah? Or Father Matthew who falls asleep at prayer? Am I the Messiah?' But puzzled as they were, they never repeated the saying again.

As time went by, the monks began to treat one another with a special love and reverence. There was a gentle, whole-hearted, human quality about them now which was hard to describe but easy to see. They lived with each other as those who had finally found something of significance. Their words were carefully considered and gentle. Who could tell when they might be speaking to the Messiah?

Before long, the vitality of the monastery attracted many visitors and young men began asking to join the community. The old hermit died without revealing any more, and the abbot sometimes wondered if he had understood correctly.

If we treat each other with respect, if we listen to each other's stories and forgive each other, there may be some hope of community. It is such a vulnerable hope, so ridiculous in the face of the new society, that I find it hard to get a grip on. But I know that I need it; that without some place of belonging all my spiritual aspirations will turn to dust and be scattered by the wind. May it not come to that.

is a FRAGILE

wrapping paper, searching in vain for some sort of note, some framework with which to make sense of it.

The perfume was too tempting. Only when she had to twist the cap hard to get it off did she realize that it had a seal on it, which she had just broken. Dabbing it on her wrists and inhaling sent a shiver down her spine. The scent was so delicate, so fragile, so complex. Any thoughts of ringing the courier company to see who it was really meant for vanished with the broken seal. She wasn't going to be accused of stealing.

She looked at the tickets. A good band, not one of her

Music

In a forest under the shelter of a great mountain, there lived a flock of beautifully coloured birds. They communicated with each other by clicking their beaks. On clear blue days, their favourite pastime was to fly high into the sky and then plummet like a stone towards the earth. One bird in particular was something of an outcast. Her plumage had somehow been distorted at birth, so that she had colours in all the wrong places. In order to win favour with the others,

Sometimes I have a day that really jams me up. I come home all anally retentive and ready for a massacre. There's only one thing to do: hit the volume button on the stereo.

If'n you don't move your feet, You won't recognize the beat.

Music. What the hell is it? How does it get on the inside when it comes from outside? Why does my mood shift when I let it in? How could anyone be human without it?

favourites, but worth listening to. This weekend. Be dumb not to go. Even if it wasn't meant for her, getting a gift lifted her spirit. There's so little in life that's free. 'Look, Patrick. Somebody loves me, you see.'

On the way to the pub, Vincent passed a beggar. Of course we don't call them beggars—what is it? 'A homeless person' will do. Very PC. This is no new experience. He probably passes two or three on the way to work every morning. But this time it hits

she set out to outdo them in the

plummeting game. Great status was

gained according to how high a bird

could reach, and how fast the ensuing

swoop to earth. So she spent hours

musicmusicmusicmusic

upon hours away on her own, practising.

Eventually there came a clear blue day,

and she knew the time was ripe. Amidst

much sniggering from the other birds,

she set out to climb into the skies. As

they watched her, she flew higher and

higher and higher. To their amazement,

she flew higher than any other bird had

him for some reason, like a tow-bar on the shins. He has to sit down nearby to recover. What's happening to me?

It's what? The incongruity of me walking past this guy, and him sitting there with the bowl. Okay, so maybe he's doing drugs or an alcoholic or doesn't want to work or something. But so what? Why him and not me? How did it happen? Is there any way out? Vincent knows the Buddhist answer (in theory at least) to suffering. Suffering comes from the illusion of self, of that little basket around which everything coheres. Ditch the basket and you ditch the problem.

ever flown. Her wings were becoming

weak, and she was running out of air to

fly through. But still she went further,

upward and onward, seeking to push

beyond all limits. It was when she was

utterly exhausted that she heard

musicmusicmusicmusi

something. It was the most piercingly

beautiful sound that she had ever heard.

As she looked around, she saw bird-like

creatures, all white. They had their

mouths open, and from their throats

came wave after wave of something

quite exquisite. The bird was caught up

But what about this guy, huh? Is it because of his desire for material existence that he has his little bowl? Should I advise him to just accept his place, to be at peace with whatever comes? I don't think so. And is the suffering his problem or my problem? If I'm the one worrying about it, I guess it must be mine.

Partly because of his confusion, partly from curiosity, Vincent does an extraordinary thing. He wanders across and sits on the footpath next to the beggar. Who stinks, frankly, this close up.

in the grandeur of it for some minutes.

So much so that she forgot to fly.

musicmusicmusicmusic

She began to fall, and the traces of

sound grew fainter. Faster and faster

she went, straining her beak forward to

slice into the air. The birds below were

astounded as a flashing meteorite came

into sight from where their eyes had lost

her. It was the most spectacular free fall

ever, and it set their beaks clicking in

delight. But as the hurtling bird reached

the end of her run, she found that she

was going too fast to be able to pull up.

'Piss off.' Not a great start. Vincent can see he's about the same age.

'Take it easy, brother, I just want to talk.'

'I'm not your bastard brother.' He reaches down and rattles the bowl. Vincent, finally understanding, digs in his pocket and puts some money in. He is rewarded with a grunt.

'How's business?'

'Not bad, you know, though I'm a bit worried about me

She strained her wings against the air,

but only succeeded in slowing her fall

slightly. She crashed through the trees

and ended up stunned upon the ground.

musicmusicmusicmusi

The other birds gathered around,

concerned. She staggered to her feet and

looked at them. But all she could think

of was the beautiful sound she had

heard before she fell. She opened her

beak, and the sound on the inside of her

became a song, causing the surrounding

birds to shiver in their feathers.

share portfolio. What do you want, mate? If you're looking for a boy you're in the wrong street.'

'No, no. Look, I'm sorry, I know this is crazy but I just want to talk. I wondered where you're from, how you got to be here.'

'What's it to you? Who are you? You a cop or something?'

'I'm just another human being, you know? Just another dumb-bum stumbling around the face of the planet trying to understand it. If you don't want to talk, that's okay, it was one more stupid thing I've done today.'

Soon they were all learning to make the

haunting and beautiful sound in their

throats. This is the way in which music

came to the earth, when an ugly bird

made the mistake of flying too high.

'You got any smokes?'

'Got some tobacco.'

'That'll do. Roll us one, will ya? Me fingers are a bit stiff. Don't bother with them filter things, mate. Might as well do the job properly if ya gonna do it at all.'

'I'm Vincent.'

'Robbie.'

'Where you from, Robbie?'

'Ah, up north, you know, a long time back. Thanks, mate.'

Treble Clef Palette

1 ounce of compassion

1 teaspoon tears of a fresh widow

1 overflowing cup of longing

A heartful of unrequited love

Half-cup of ecstasy

2 fistfuls of quavers, crotchets etc.

Blend ingredients to produce a marinade.

Soak for a few decades, basting regularly.

The mixture is ready to use when it begins to bubble and can no longer be held in container.

Ladle liberally over ears (see earlier recipe for Listanga).

Chill, baby, chill.

They sit in silence for a few moments sharing the nicotine communion.

'So how'd you end up on the streets?'

'I left school and did me trade as a typesetter, see? In the days when they used to use real type. Then the whole thing changed; they started switching to computers. I was stuffed—couldn't understand how to turn one on, let alone operate it. Lost me job, nothing else I was qualified for. I was married, but I started bashing me wife. She took off with someone else, I hit the bottle, here I am.'

Who
makes the
music-maker
?

'How long have you been doing this?'

'Two years, on and off. Don't look so po-faced about it—it's not a bad life, you know. I still draw the dole, don't waste anything on accommodation, plenty left to have a few drinks.'

'But what are you planning to do? What about the future?'

'I leave that to blokes like you, mate. I just take one day at a time, you know what I mean? Live for the present, that's me.'

'The eternal now.'

Doesn't it strike you as strange that some people can spend their whole life studying music, get degrees and everything, and yet they still can't hear it? Still can't dance? And then there's others, never studied anything other than the way that people laugh, and they can play guitar like their fingers were on fire?

Maybe music is the breath of God, breezing out through the universe, pleading for some harmonies. Whatever. It feeds my soul, stokes my heart, gives my psyche a righteous-good massage. All kinds of music are good for the journey: hip-hop, trip-hop, garage, Indy, retro-rock, techno, ambient, whatever. Even that screechy-waily stuff they call opera.

In the beginning was the Singer... ...and the Song goes on.

'Say what?'

'Robbie, mate, this life is full of shit.'

'I'll drink to that.' And from somewhere, like a master magician, he is producing the proverbial bottle in a brown paper bag, waving it aggressively under Vincent's nose. The thick sweet smell of sherry causes his eyes to shut, but Vincent takes a swig anyway. He hands the bottle back to Robbie, who is taking a longer pull. A woman with a shopping trolley humphs as she trundles past.

If you can't find the music in your heart, then you're never going to hear the music in the world. The one beat leads on to the other. Too many people never got round to listening for the music. The Singer and the Song need each other. It's in partnership that music is made. Everyone has to know their part if the thing is going to happen.

The Pied Piper played a mean saxophone.

The rhythm of life has a powerful beat...

Vincent puts his hand on Robbie's shoulder, and hoists himself to his feet. There are things he needs to be doing, and this isn't one of them.

#

The day started well. The sun slanted through her window and crawled up the wall. In some parallel universe the birds on the roof were ecstatic and noisy. The journey into consciousness had been delicious, with none of the usual dream aftertaste. This was a gifted day. Meeting Paula and finding their way to

the outdoor concert venue was hassle-free. There was only the faintest edge of panic when she presented the tickets at the gate. Paula, who had a stubborn practical streak through her weirdness, had brought a blanket to sit on. And some food.

The sun made everyone relax. It was not, like, a heavy atmosphere, you know? Paula put it down to a combination of favourable alignment of the planets and her personal bio-rhythms, which she had just had done. Marilyn was inclined to give some credit to the righteous weed which they had shared, and which was creating a sweet microclimate over the venue.

For a long time the people waited in the hall for the arrival of the famous Rabbi. They were anxious to have the opportunity to ask their special questions of this wise man. Eventually he arrived, and was ushered up on to the stage. He looked out at the people, sensing their eager-ness for answers. After a time he began to hum a haunting melody. Before long people began humming along, such

Some vaguely techno music was interrupted by roadies and their predictable 'Check, check.' Marilyn felt herself to be at the centre of some great and endless calm, an emotional anticyclone, stationary over her state.

The security guy at the gate wants to search his bag. And frisk him.

'Ooh—how about doing it again, this time with feeling?'

Behind the shades there is a scowl of contempt, and a firm

was the tune. The Rabbi burst into song,

and everyone sang with him. Next he

began to dance, moving with very careful

measured steps. The crowd could not

help themselves; they began to move

with him. Soon everyone was dancing

and singing, and oblivious to anything

else in the universe, so caught up were

they in the Rabbi's song. It was a long

time later that the dance slowed and

hand on the back to propel Vincent out of consideration. He's on his own, straight, looking forward to the music. The thing about music is that it can take you out of yourself, take you out of the pain and the boredom. In a world where no one speaks your language, music is like coming home. Getting down at a concert is the closest thing to a spiritual experience, you know?

He is fussy about position. You have to get yourself in the right place to make the most of the sounds. He is a snob when it comes to music, élitist to the core. He scans the crowd with disdain, noting how many of them are in bad places. He walks

came to a halt. The Rabbi looked out

on the radiant faces. Only then did he

speak, and only one sentence: 'I trust,'

he said, 'that I have answered all your

questions.'

through them, watching, sensing, listening. At last he is satisfied, and sits in a small gap between two blankets. The balance is good. He looks around, half hoping that someone will have noticed the care with which he chose his position. But he is among the ignorati, who have no appreciation of these important matters.

There's a couple of hours to go before the main band. He plays a game of stories. It's simple. Pick a person, and imagine the details of their life. It's all there, in their faces. The trick is to read it. He starts with a woman in a denim jacket, with long

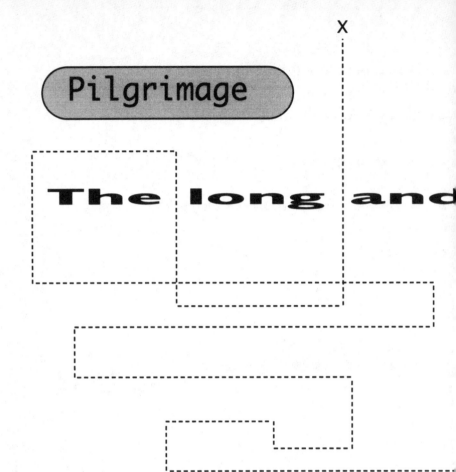

Pilgrimage

The long and

blonde hair and a hardness around her eyes. Looks to be around 30 and has on a pair of snakeskin boots.

Her name would be Cynthia. She grew up in a small rural town. Her father owned the local garage, and always had grease under his nails and the smell of barrier cream about him. Her mother had been a schoolteacher, but had stopped work after she had children. Cynthia has happy childhood memories. She was a bit of a tomboy, loved climbing trees and building huts. She had two older brothers, and her father loved her more than any. He was putty in her hands. Her mother was a little

Who remembers where they came from anymore? Let alone where we're heading to. Our lives have as much direction as an ant on amphetamines. And yet everyone is talking journey. Seems we can't get over the notion that we're moving from someplace to someplace else. I mean, even getting lost in the back streets is a journey, right?

The idea of pilgrimage is kind of ancient. At certain times (only the pilgrim

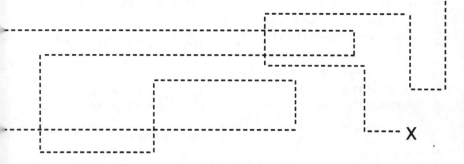

winding road...

knows the time), there comes the call to head for a special place. Maybe it's not clear at the outset where that place is, or how to get there. Maybe the place doesn't exist. But once you hear the call, you either start moving or you die. There's different types of journeys. Some of them are sacred.

jealous of this closeness, and would sometimes be hard on Cynthia so as to get her own back.

There was only one school in the town, that everyone went to. At the age of 15, Cynthia was raped in the back seat of a car by a sports jock who everyone admired. Her friends told her not to be so bloody stupid, anyone would be glad to be blocked by him. She never told her father. Life changed for her. She worked for a while after school at a hamburger bar. One day she had enough, and left for the city. Her parents and brothers could never understand why she left.

It's a mistake to think that the destination is the most important part. The most insufferable people are those who think they've arrived, and trade their shoes for a comfortable bed. A coffin is very comfortable. We were made with the hunger for the road in our gut. Best to face it. Travellers are different from other people. They have a faraway look in their eye. They don't carry too much stuff because they know it will weigh them down. They have trouble settling. When they do stop for a while, they like to swap stories with fellow travellers. People on the road recognize each other. It's just this pilgrimage thing.

What can we do? We were born with the Great Unrest. Our father taught us that life is one long journey on which only the unfit are left behind.

CARIBOU ESKIMO

After a rough patch she met a guy in the office she worked in, and moved in with him. She was happy, and dreamed of marriage and kids.

One night at a party, she got drunk and ended up kissing some guy she had only just met. Her partner found them and, after beating the guy turned on her. She had her nose broken— you can still see the bump now if you look closely. It was the end of the relationship, the only long-term one Cynthia has had thus far. She majors on one-nighters, and has become pretty cynical about men. That's Cynthia.

Jesus was a sailor when he walked upon the water and he spent a long time watching from his lonely wooden tower and when he knew for certain only drowning men could see him he said all men will be sailors then until the sea shall free them...

LEONARD COHEN

When I rest my feet my mind also ceases to function. J.G. HAMANN

There's this golden glow spreading from the inside of me. I don't know if it's the weed or the day. The only problem is something hard under my shoulder which is making itself felt even through the blanket. That's better. Paula is chattering about something or other. The woman who does Shiatsu for her, and who reads Tarot on the side. I'm trying to concentrate, put the right responses in the right places, but I'm not sure that it's working. Paula won't mind. She's happy talking. I'm drifting

At times I get sick of moving, you know how it is? Tired of being on the way somewhere when all around me there are people dug in for the duration and doing very nicely. Nostalgic for all the places I've left behind for the sake of the ones remaining unexplored. Just wanting to be **normal**. But it passes.

If there is any meaning to life in the cyber-tundra, then it's to be found on the way between here and somewhere else.

Pioneers are people who go places no one else has been before. I've got the wanderlust in my heart, and it's burning, baby.

I once met a man coming back from the place I was heading to. He advised me to go no further. He told me of the dangers and difficulties I would face if I persevered. I thanked him for his advice, and ignored it. Later on in my travels I suffered the troubles he had warned me of. I regretted nothing.

across the face of the earth, riding on the sweet breeze which makes my hair tickle my face.

There's this pulsating buzzing thang happening here. I'm not sure I know what it is, and yet it seems to register way back in the memory banks somewhere. I know this feeling, but I can't remember how to label it anymore. And then it hits me, and I must have gasped because Paula has stopped her rant to look at me. It's life! That's what it is. Life coursing through my body, seeping up through the earth, pouring down from the sky, murmuring in the humanity all around. Life. And it feels good.

I'm on my Way...

'Nothing,' I say to Paula, and she carries on with whatever it is she's on to now.

Take that guy over there. Big guy with a singlet and a tat on his upper arm. Must be called something like Steve. Steve lived his early years in a block of council flats which looked like they belonged in Moscow. To this day the smell of urine reminds him of his childhood.

He never had a father that he knew of. His mother had

2 Two roads diverged in a yellow wood,
And sorry I could not travel both
And be one traveller, long I stood
And looked down one as far as I could
To where it bent in the undergrowth;
Then took the other, as just as fair,
And having perhaps the better claim,
Because it was grassy and wanted wear;
Though as for that the passing there
Had worn them really about the same,
And both that morning equally lay
In leaves no step had trodden black.
Oh, I kept the first for another day!
Yet knowing how way leads on to way,
I doubted if I should ever come back.
I shall be telling this with a sigh
Somewhere ages and ages hence:
Two roads diverged in a wood, and I—
I took the one less travelled by,
And that has made all the difference.

ROBERT FROST

two boys, both by different fathers, neither of whom she lived with. She was a tough old bird, his Mum, and everyone in the flats was scared of her tongue. She could strip the skin off you without ever touching you.

The one thing Steve had going for him was his size. The tough world he lived in taught him to use it well. He always had a lot of friends and not too many enemies. There was a legendary story that he had picked a guy up and thrown him off a second floor balcony. Actually he had just punched the guy and he fell over the rail. Steve was sick to the pit of his stomach

A certain woman knew herself to be dying, and so set out on a journey to discover the meaning of life. It turned out to be a long and adventurous trip. One day she met another woman coming towards her on the path.

'Where are you headed?' she asked this stranger.

'I am on a pilgrimage to find the meaning of life,' replied the woman.

'Then we are heading for the same destination. But we are travelling in opposite directions.'

'One of us must be travelling the wrong way.'

'Perhaps,' said the dying woman. 'On the other hand, each of us knows and has come from the place that the other is heading towards. Why not share our stories?'

The two women spoke long into the night. It happened that the older one breathed her last that very evening, and died in the arms of her new friend. In the morning, the lone pilgrim continued her journey. But it was no longer quite as difficult or frightening.

And before I'd be a slave I'll be buried in my grave And go home to my Lord And be free.

OLD SPIRITUAL

after; he though he'd killed the guy; but he'd landed on a pile of cardboard boxes waiting for the rubbish and was okay. But it didn't do Steve's rep any harm.

He was no good at school. He sat in the too small desks and hated it, all the words and ideas flying past. Only when the bell rang and it was interval did he find anything that he could make sense of. The girls were impressed with his size and strength. Sometimes he would beat up some kid just for the effect it would have on the crowd. But he never knew what to do with girls. Never knew how to speak to them without

May the breeze be ever at your back; May the road rise up to meet you.

swearing or frightening them. As a teenager he would hire dirty vids and jack himself off, washing his hand afterwards to try to get rid of the smell.

He got a job as a plumber's apprentice, and did well. They all liked him, the guys did. He could drink beer like there was no tomorrow, and still stand on his feet. But even though they joked with him and teased him, they were scared of him too. Steve didn't have too many friends, except for one scrawny guy, Brian, who took an interest in him. Brian and Steve worked together on a lot of jobs and always got on well. When he found

There's a lot of people who take themselves too seriously. If all the accountants in the world were laid end to end, they'd be much happier people. Subcommittees are evidence that hell may exist.

Get a LIFE

out Brian was gay, he couldn't believe it at first. Then he felt betrayed and angry. He ignored him, had nothing to do with him for almost a year.

The news of the AIDS made him think again. He visited Brian on one of his stays in hospital. He took him some chocolate, worried that flowers might give the wrong idea. Brian cried, and Steve didn't know what to do. Later, on his own, he cried himself. He cursed his big clumsy body and the lack of words to describe what was happening inside. After the funeral he went to the pub and picked a fight with a huge

If you're not having fun somewhere, then it's not happening. We can make machines that know how to **work**— only humans (and animals) know to

Come out

play. If there is a God who made us, then he was only looking for play-mates. You can bet he wasn't thinking of pedants who get excited by balance sheets. I mean to say, contemplate an aardvark.

and

play

Irishman who obligingly beat Steve to a pulp. These days Steve is looking for a woman, to reassure him that he's not queer. That's Steve.

There's some part of the world that's changed. Then I twigged. Paula wasn't talking. I sit up to see what's happened, and she's gone. I have this vague recollection of her asking something about the toilet, and me grunting. The crowd has really packed in, a patchwork of people. There's a second-rate band doing

Unless you become

Nobody teaches children how to play. They appear to arrive with the software pre-packaged. It's as natural as breathing. The problem is when the capacity for play gets lost/repressed/prohibited.

Play

Ploy

Plot

Blot

Boot

Loot

Lost

like a *child* you will never enter the place you are looking for.

---

the opening, and some punters with no taste dancing to it down the front. I'm feeling very mellow and loose in the jaw. It's good wearing no bra, and feeling my boobs relax against the cotton of my dress. The breeze sneaks into the sleeveless armholes and caresses me like no man ever could.

I throw my head back and let the sun warm my sun-blocked face. In these poxy ozone-depleted times. I should have brought Patrick with me. But it's a bit risky at a thing like this, and it's not like he can look after himself. I tune into the band, trying to snatch some lyrics out of the disharmony.

Ideas for play:

1

The only people that matter are the ones who want to play.

3 **2** Get as dirty as you possibly can.

Play with your whole body.

4 The playground has no boundaries.

5 Try not to hurt anyone, including yourself.

> *There's no other day than the one I'm in;*
> *There's no body else who will fit my skin;*
> *I'm an only child, I'm a lonely child,*
> *I'm an orphan who's conceived in sin.*

I catch a hint of that perfume wafting from where I have dabbed it. Once again it catches me by surprise, and it threatens to make me cry. Whoever sent that stuff to me, thanks be to your anonymous self.

I've got this feeling like someone's watching me. You know how it is?

I used to be a lot older than I am now. In those days I would keep off the grass and eat boiled cabbage and always flush. Life was a serious business and we all had responsibilities blah blah blah... Since then I've grown down a lot. I get wet in the rain and go barefoot even when it burns my feet. I dance in my uniquely uncoordinated way, and I couldn't care less if people laugh at me. I draw pictures with tomato sauce on my food. I fill condoms with water, and throw them at prudes. I have unprotected music, and don't even think about the possibility of AIDS in my ears. I rip insignificant articles out of the newspaper so that people will wonder what had been there that was of interest. I make kites that never fly, but I have a lot of fun dragging them along the grass in anticipation. I blow raspberries on babies' tummies and kiss old women on the lips. I fart in the bath and pray a lot. I wonder what I will be when I have really grown down.

# #

Now that one's a bit more of a challenge. She has thick black hair, cropped at the base of her neck. A simple sleeveless sunfrock. Her legs apart, her face tipped back, as if she's being ravished by the sun. I'll call her Susan. She was born to a sixteen-year-old working-class girl, who was forced to adopt her out. Susan was a beautiful baby, so there was no trouble finding parents for her. The couple who were selected had been infertile for five long years of trying. She was an accounts

In the beginning there was the game. But there weren't enough players. So God made some. First off they had a lot of fun.

Play Then some of the players got angry with each other. They got to shouting and throwing things around the place.

for Some of them started cheating. In the end they all wandered off and started doing other things. The players all

~~keeps~~

peeks

thought what they were doing was much more **important** than games.

---

manager in a photography business, and he was a shipping clerk. They were so happy.

A year later, she fell pregnant. It was such a shock they could hardly believe it. She had a boy, whom they named Peter. They still loved Susan, but it was not quite the same as your own flesh and blood. Susan, as a toddler, suffered from the lack of attention and started to develop behaviour problems. Which made things worse all round. By the time she reached adolescence, she hated her parents with a passion. When she found out she had been adopted, it all made sense but it made

Play without

ceasing...

God was left alone. So he invented children. But they kept turning into adults.

So he kept on having to make new ones, which meant the place got pretty crowded. Still, at least there was someone to play with.

THE APOSTLE PAUL (NEARLY)

her angry and bitter as well. She started doing drugs, stopped going to school and eventually left home. Her parents were relieved.

She got a job as a wp operator in an insurance firm. Her office manager was in his thirties, a fat guy with bad breath. He would lean over her shoulder and pretend to be looking at what was on the screen. When he called her into his office and shut the door she knew what was coming. She didn't resist because it seemed somehow easier to go along with it, and at least she would keep her job. But she spent a good hour in the

We are bodies.

ankle finger stretch stomach ear nose lip toe
tongue lick skin eye tip nostril thumb shin
thigh teeth heel throat pulse hair cheek
ejaculate elbow navel suck shoulder brow

Sexuality

scrotum calf sole hip
ache armpit buttock
knee tickle forearm breast wrist chin leg scalp
back palm saliva stroke ovary bone orgasm
synapse neck vein foreskin chest voice jaw
muscle pelvis lobe nipple loin head bosom

shower afterwards. He was at her all the time after that, and in the end she left, but not before putting a fresh dog turd in the drawer of his desk.

Susan has been doing temp work since then, enjoying the variety. In the evenings she has been doing a photography course, and it turns out she's quite good at it. It's her little secret, which she keeps from everyone. She loves to be alone in the darkroom, watching the images appear out of nowhere. She keeps everyone away from this one enjoyable creative part of her life, for fear they will damage it. There's an unusual

belly vagina knuckle excrete face rump sinew
hear lash wrinkle eyelid orifice testicle pore
stubble scratch odour temple penis blood tissue
hold nerve labia organ tingle member glans
caress sweat heart digestion tibia canal iris
skull brain clitoris gum marrow pectoral taste
flesh lung hamstring breath massage pubis
smell arch fondle forehead sting follicle eat
womb groin see spine cell gland pupil tonsil
sperm pigment freckle liver throb spleen kiss
limb pimple

Bodies are good.

mixture of fear and trust in her eyes. Is that what it is?
That's Susan.

# #

The support band is getting toward the end of its act, thank
God. I wonder how long a break they're going to have? And
what's happened to Paula? That guy is staring at me. Not like
he's perving or coming on; more like he's trying to work me
out. Interesting looking guy, sort of thoughtful. He's got a
friendly open face, like he doesn't have too much to hide.

Bodies

go

Bodies are good for a whole lot of stuff. **Sex** is more fun than most other things you can think of. I almost always prefer it to jogging or cutting my toe-nails. Unfortunately it is almost always harder to arrange than the alternatives, and a lot more complicated. Some

Skinny as. Damn. I think he's seen me looking. I don't want any hassles today. ... *A cloud drifts briefly across the face of the sun.* ... Which is a real pity, because it's made her tip her head forward again. Like a flower closing up when the sun disappears. I'll swear she was eyeing me back. She's quite gorgeous, not in the pretty sense, but with a depth of spirit or something. Have I got the energy for any more relationships? I'll have to stop watching or she'll think I'm a creep. ... *A guy is wandering past selling filled rolls, picking his way among the crowd.* ... I think I must be hungry. In fact I'm damn sure of it. But I put

are od ✓

people think that sex has nothing to do with spirituality, but then some people think that life is about money. Go figure. Sex is a fully engaged form of love. Sex without love is like eating without appreciation. It can be done, but what's the point of it? It's possible to fritter away your humanity in banal bonking. The worst thing is, you might mistake it for love. Bonking instead of love is to imagine that a candle is basically the same thing as the sun.

my money in Paula's purse, and she's gone off with it. Great, that's the sun back. How many days do you get in a life when you feel as good as this? How could I have been so depressed such a short time ago? With this much light it's hard to believe in shadows.

Is there any meaning to it? Or is it just a random pattern of light and darkness that you have no control over? I woke up this morning and the shadow had shifted. But why? It's not like I had done anything different. It just happened. Which means that tomorrow I might wake up and find it's back again. Oh,

1+1

I don't want to fake love any more

Loving sexuality is wonderful stuff. There is a tenderness and mutuality about it. At the point of climax the ego-boundaries come as close to collapse as they're ever likely to get. It's possible to lose a sense of where you stop and the other starts.

well. Today I'm happy and the sun is shining and there's music out there and I'm going to enjoy it. I wonder if that guy is still looking? Perhaps just a sneaky glance. Yes. ... *There's a Mexican wave started while the crowd waits for what they've come for.* ... I just can't keep my eyes off her. I don't think she is a Susan after all. What then? Initiating conversations between strangers. It's such a game, so bloody pathetic. Every line's as lame as the next, every word as insincere. 'How long do you think the band will be?' 'I haven't seen hair quite as black as yours.' 'Did you choose this spot because of the sound?' 'Have you ever considered

The two shall become **one**

$$= 2 = 1$$

skydiving naked?' I'm a complete flop at this sort of thing.
I wish I was a bit more extroverted. The trouble is the more
you think about it, the more nervous you get. I've watched
guys cruise up and slip into it so naturally that no one knows
that anything is happening. But that first line—that floater—
it's an invitation to disaster. Everything, all of you, offered out
there to take or refuse. I've been shredded by experts. Cut so
deeply that it's taken me weeks to get over it. So do I risk it?
Is it worth it?

'You've got beautiful feet.' There it is, before he can stop it.

Sex is about intimacy. It's about being naked and vulnerable in the presence of another person. There is no going back once the boundaries have been passed. It is a risky business. You lay yourself open. There is no such thing as 'safe' sex: the whole thing is highly dangerous. If there is trust and compassion; if there is gentleness and consideration; if there is passion and adventure; if there is intimacy and responsibility: then sex is a sign of God. It is a preparation for learning how to love with everything you have. Good sex has a sacrality about it, because it is a discovery of the depths of mystery of a human being. Sex is for enjoyment: enjoy...

Love **Gone** **Lone** **Bone** **Bonk** **Bunk** **Busk** **Bust** **Lust**

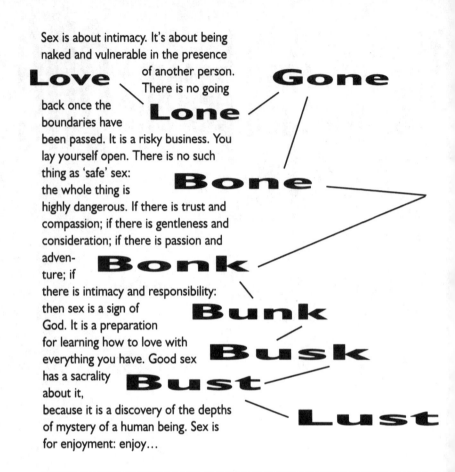

'I beg your pardon?'

'Sorry, but I've just been admiring your feet. They're lovely. People don't pay much attention to feet, but they tell you a lot about a person.'

'Oh really? And what do my feet tell you about me?' Smiling with the sun.

'Well your feet tell me that you own a blind parakeet named George, and that you don't play hopscotch on a regular basis.'

awe

When my beloved first stands before me naked, all open to my sight, there is a feeling throughout the whole of me; Why? If sex is no more than an instinct, why don't I simply feel horny or hungry?... Why awe? Why should sex be complicated by reverence?

M. SCOTT PECK

'That's my cousin, Carol, you're thinking of. I'm the one who doesn't play chess.'

'Oh yes, I see that now. It's the way I'm sitting—I forgot for a moment which hemisphere I'm in. Easy to mix up the left and the right foot, and then you get a completely different story. I'm Vincent.'

'Marilyn. Would you like to come and sit over here just to get the right perspective on my feet? Or is that being a bit forward?'

When mystics and other pioneers of the divine heartland describe their encounters with God, they often use sexual analogies. Why? **Where →** Because sex is the best illustration they can find for what happens. It's a kind of cosmic orgasm. Which means that loving sexuality between people is good practice. Not everything to do with spirituality has to be hard work.

Love is, God

is

'It's an acceptable risk, as they say in Muroroa. Thanks. That's better. Now I can see quite clearly that you drink Earl Grey tea with a slice of lemon, and that you're not wearing any shoes.'

'Absolutely amazing. I don't suppose you'll tell me how you do it?'

'My Greek uncle threatened to stitch my mouth closed if I ever gave away the secret. The rest of you is quite lovely as well.'

Sex is not about genitals and sweat, though they come into it. It's about respect, dignity, patience, trust, intimacy, surrender, pleasuring, embrace, consideration, ecstasy, sensuality and love. And the greatest of these is love.

You would know the Lord's meaning in this thing? Know it well. Love was the meaning. Who showed it you? Love. What did God show you? Love. Why were you shown it? For love. Hold on to this and you will know and understand love more and more. But you will not know or learn anything else— ever. So it was that I learned that love was God's meaning. And I saw for certain, both here and elsewhere, that before we were ever made, God loved us; and that this love has never slackened, nor ever shall. In this love all works have been done, and in this love God has made everything serve us; and in this love our life is everlasting. Our beginning was when we were made, but the love in which we were made never had beginning. In it we have our beginning.

JULIAN OF NORWICH DESCRIBES HER VISION OF GOD

Lust is the craving for salt of a man who is dying of thirst...
FREDERICK BUECHNER

'You can stay, Vincent. I don't suppose you've got any money on you?'

'Enough to buy a sandwich but not enough for a car.'

'Perfect. Only my friend's gone off with my money, and I'm dead hungry. If I could just borrow the price of a filled roll till she gets...'

'You're the first person who's wanted me for my money, Marilyn. I'd be glad to help those feet in any way possible.' And the light is shining in the darkness.

Crossing Boundaries

How does it happen, this separation thing? When I was very young, kids were just kids. We somehow missed the fact that it was important what colour they were or how they spoke or where they came from. Along the way somewhere, things changed.

Paula finds the pair of them, eating and very friendly. Not that she minds. It's hard to imagine that Marilyn would combine business and pleasure, so she must be genuinely interested in this guy. Rather yummy that he is. Introductions all round, as they make enough room for three on the blanket. Vincent manages to persuade Paula to have the last half of his roll.

'What sign are you, Vincent?' Paula finds it hard to relax until she has some basic information about a person.

EMTHEMTHEMTHEMTHEMTHEMTHEMTHEMTHEI
EMTHEMTHEMTHEMTHEMTHEMTHEMTHEMTHEI
EMTHEMTHEMTHEMTHEMTHEMTHEMTHEMTHEI
EMTHEMTHEMTHEMTHEMTHEMTHEMTHEMTHEI
EMTHEMTHEMTHEMTHEMTHEMTHEMTHEMTHEI
EMTHEMTHEMTHEMTHEMTHEMTHEMTHEMTHEI
EMTHEMTHEMTHEM**USUS**THEMTHEMTHEI
EMTHEMTHEMTHEM**USUS**THEMTHEMTHEI
EMTHEMTHEM**USUSUSUSUS**THEMTHEI
EMTHEMTHEM**USUSUSUSUS**THEMTHEI
EMTHEMTHEM**USUS**THEMTHEMTHEI
EMTHEMTHEM**USUS**THEMTHEI
EMTHEMTHEMTHEMTHEMTHEMTHEMTHEI
EMTHEMTHEMTHEMTHEMTHEMTHEMTHEI

'Gemini. Are you into astrology?'

'I'm into whatever makes sense of life, my boy, and the stars are certainly in that camp. What date's your birthday?'

'May 24.'

'On the cusp, yes, that figures.'

'Do I pass?'

'You'll do, Vincent.'

'Anyway,' says Marilyn, 'back to me.'

'Sorry, darling. I wouldn't take your boy off you—you

We do things the right way. It's not something that anyone had to teach us. We just grew up understanding that this is the way things are. People like us are easy to relate to. We understand the stuff we're talking about. When we're together, we don't have to explain ourselves. We laugh at each other's jokes. It's not surprising that we like to hang out with each other and eat the sort of food we all enjoy. I don't know why people find it hard to join us. We're a very accepting group.

know that. I'm just trying to protect you.'

The noise of the crowd and rush of bodies toward the front presage the first wonderfully jarring guitar chord slicing through the crowd. There won't be any conversation for a while.

#

That night Vincent is lying on his bed in the warm air. He is wondering what this new intrusion means for his life. These things just come out of left field. All of a sudden there is a

They do things differently. They talk funny and eat strange foods and wear weird clothes. To be honest, they even smell different. They don't really make much effort to learn the right way of doing things. They THEM **seem to prefer their own company; they're always hanging around together. If only they could make a bit of an effort to integrate, they might be easier to relate to. They don't seem to understand that they put people off by being so strange.**

person in your life who wasn't there before, and everything is different. You lose all power of rational thought. Every time Vincent tries to work through this logically and think about the implications of a relationship, and commitment, all he can see is those feet and that hair and the eyes. Which is of no practical help at all. And the smell. The scent of her, the deeper aroma of woman, the smell of her hair. Where is your cynicism when you need it? Where is the self-protective egotism that keeps people in their place, on the outside of the circle?

The cat is not getting his full attention tonight. But

If things are ever going to change, somebody has to take the risk of crossing the boundaries that keep us apart. There's too much hatred, mistrust, suspicion, prejudice; and it hurts us all.

and genocide. The agenda for peace and reconciliation begins in the human heart. It will only succeed when it begins amongst groups of ordinary people who are different from each other, but still want to live together.

We are One

It's too easy to live in our hermetically sealed cells of isolation. This is the time for breakout. This is the age in which the walls come down. Each of us is going to have to go beyond what makes us comfortable if we are going to put the human back into humanity. Crossing boundaries is no easy thing. It demands courage and commitment. But the alternative is unthinkable. The petty prejudice we find in our hearts is the seed which blossoms into warfare

Vincent doesn't give a toss. There is some magic in the air, some sparkling mystery falling like glitter into the dull expanse of his existence, and he's not going to be the one to resist it. And all the colours seem to be so much brighter than he remembers them.

    'Perhaps there is a God after all,' he says to himself. And then realizes that he has spoken out loud.

Hope is so fragile that sometimes you feel like smashing it yourself to save the anxiety. Marilyn is hanging by a thread.

A† THE LINES...

... things look different. When you cross the boundary and look back from the other side, a lot becomes clear for the first time. But first, you have to leave where you are and move into somebody else's territory.

Jesus Christ said he had never been to a football match.

So we took him to one, my friends and I. It was a ferocious battle between the Protestant Punchers and the Catholic Crusaders. The Crusaders scored first. Jesus cheered wildly and threw his hat high up in the air.

She is remembering a time when her mother bought her a canary and a birdcage. The bird was so yellow. Like someone had carved it out of butter. And it would sing in clear pure tones. She thought it the most beautiful creature in all the world. The song of the canary almost seemed to Marilyn like it came from a different world.

She heard a story once about how a bird had flown all the way to heaven, where it had heard angelic music. The bird couldn't last long there, and eventually fell back to earth. But the music was remembered, and the bird sang the song—

Then the Punchers scored. And

Jesus cheered wildly and threw

his hat up in the air. This seemed to puzzle the man behind us.

He tapped Jesus on the shoulder and asked,

'Which side are you

supporting, my good

man?' 'Me?' replied Jesus, all excited, 'I'm not going

for either side. I'm just enjoying the game.' The questioner

turned to his neighbour and

sneered, 'Hmm, an atheist!'

a piece of heaven. She was sure that her canary was that bird.

She fed and pampered the bird, refusing to name it because there were no names good enough. She would clean the cage without any prompting from her mother. And then one day she came home to find her father trying to teach the canary swear words. She could not believe it—filthy curses being spoken to this divine bird. Marilyn ran from the room crying, and neither of her parents ever understood what she was upset about. It was then that Marilyn decided that the bird would have to go free. She could not bear to have something so

With his own body he broke down the wall that separated them and kept them enemies.

Maybe that's what it takes. That we lay ourselves on the line so that other people can cross over. There's any number of boundaries; there's not so many people willing to cross them.

beautiful destroyed by that man. So she planned to release it from the cage. But it was hard for her to let go of the only thing she truly loved. She kept putting it off and putting it off.

Finally she decided that there was no choice. That day when she came home from school, she would sneak the canary out of the cage and release it to fly away over the housetops. Except that when she got home, the bird was dead in the bottom of the cage. Her mother said later that it had probably been frightened by a cat and died of a heart attack. Marilyn was never sure. She cried in her room for hours on end.

L

o

v

e

genderclassagesexualorientatic

It is clear that Vincent represents a threat to my world. I have taken so much time and effort to put things in their place. But what a wonderful way to have them unsettled. And she is giggling and trembling at the same time.

#

They meet in a small café. Marilyn has chosen it, careful to find a place where she will not be known. The wine is not too bad, and does its thing. Vincent is full of smart lines, but every now

olourlanguagecreedbeliefrace

and again he catches her eye and has to remember what he was talking about. They make it most of the way through mains without getting personal.

'I don't know much about you,' Vincent offers.

'That's probably the best way to have it. Anyway, I know nothing about you either.'

'What would you like to know?'

'I don't know: your shoe size, what you do when you're being naughty, what films you love, what sort of disgusting

aparthatedivide

A guru asked his disciples how they could aparthatedivide tell when the night

had ended and the day had begun.

One said, 'When you see an animal in the distance and

can tell whether it is a cow or a horse.'

'No,' said the guru.

aparthate divide

'When you look at a tree in the

distance and can tell if it is **a c c e p t**

eforgive an apple tree or a pear tree,'

suggested another.

---

personal habits you have, how you got your name, that sort of thing.'

'I was named after Vincent Van Gogh, because one of my ears was folded over when I was born. I've always found him a hard act to live up to. The madness is okay; it's the creative genius that stretches me.'

'Do you do anything artistic?'

'A bit of self-obsessed poetry, a few chords on the guitar, that's about it.'

'Wrong again,' said the guru.

'Well then, what is it?' asked the disciples.

aparthatedivide   'When you

look into the face of any man and recognize your brother in

him; when you look into the face of any woman and recognise

in her your sister. If you can't do this, no matter what time it is

by the sun, it is still night.'   **acceptloveforgi**

o v e f o r g i v e

acceptloveforgive

'Where do you go when you're happy?'

'To the park, usually. I go to watch the trees. I've always had a thing about trees. I like to sit in them, hold them, watch them bending in the wind. Now, it must be my turn.'

'Who says you get a turn?'

'Gender equality—it's a sign of the times. What's your favourite snack food?'

'That's easy—cashew nuts.'

'Expensive tastes. What sort of work do you do?'

Giving

Give
Live
Love

Christmas really disappoints me. If I never ate another turkey; if I never pulled another cracker and got to wear a lime-green party hat; if I never drank beer, red wine, champagne and port all in one day again; why then, the world would be a better place for all of us. But the thing that really gets me going about Christmas is the way that it trivializes giving. I mean what is this all about? Really. I don't want people beating their feet round crowded shopping centres feeling guilty because the only thing they can think to get me is another pair of underpants. I don't want to pretend to be radiantly joyous when I remove said underpants from their wrapping paper. Christmas is not about giving. It's a guilt-driven, self-indulgent, commercially manipulated pile of crap that produces flatulence and full sewers.

The problem is that it distorts what real giving is all about. Giving is something that is chosen in freedom, and it is more about lifestyle than shopping lists.

'Let's just leave that for the moment, shall we? Ask me another.' What was that he saw in her eyes? Panic, was it?

'Okay, okay. What's important to you in life?'

'Money, success, power...that sort of thing. Not.'

'So what then?'

'I'd like to find something solid and certain. Something to hold on to and believe in. I'd like to know what life's for, or if it's for anything at all. I want some **meaning**, you know? Does that sound neurotic, or what?'

x

You give but little when you give of your possessions. It is when you

KAHLIL GIBRAN

give of yourself that you truly give.

'Not. It sounds honest. I'm just having trouble here believing that I have found another human being who is willing to scratch beneath the surface of life. I've just about given up hope of anyone asking any questions at all. Most people I know only want answers.'

'Vincent, don't take this the wrong way, but are you gay?'

'No. What makes you ask that?'

'I don't know. I'm just trying to eliminate possibilities, I guess. I'm not either, just for the record.'

Lord, make me an instrument of your peace.

Where there is hatred, let me sow love;

Where there is injury, pardon;

Where there is doubt, faith;

Where there is despair, hope;

Where there is darkness, light;

And where there is sadness, joy.

In order to give you have to learn to let go. To get beyond the habit of ownership and control. Giving involves treating another person as though they are as important as yourself.

'Well, that's helped to get us past first base, hasn't it? Want some dessert?'

Walking together down the warm pavements seems the only natural thing to do. As natural as leaning into each other and holding hands. He looks up.

'Starry, starry night,' with a flourish of his free arm at the shining heavens.

O Divine Master, grant that I might not so much

seek to be consoled as to console;

To be understood as to understand;

To be loved as to love;

For it is in giving that we receive—

It is in pardoning that we are pardoned;

And it is in dying that we are born to eternal life.

She stops him, holds both hands, and sings to him in a cracked and very gentle voice:

'I could have told you, Vincent: this world was never made for one as beautiful as you.' And pressing her lips so softly on his.

They continue strolling, cocooned in something which has been growing all evening. Words retreat now, because they are taking away instead of adding. Eventually they reach the entrance to Marilyn's block of flats. This threshold over which she has led so many men. She turns to look at him.

It is better to **give** than to recede...

MOTTO OF THE BALD

You can only give once you have been given to.

'Do you want to come up?'

'Let me tell you something about myself. When I was a little boy, I wanted to grow plants. My father gave me some beans, and I planted them. They all came up, but then one by one they died before they grew much at all. So my father gave me one more bean. This time, when it came up, he showed me how to build a little shelter to protect it from the snails and the cold. It grew strong and tall, and I was able to take the shelter away.'

'Why do I have the feeling this is supposed to mean something?'

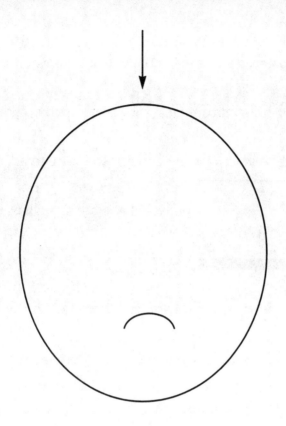

'Marilyn, would you understand if I don't come up?'

It was only then that the full terror of the possibility of love fell upon her, shaking her to the very core.

She is lying there in the dark, with the crucifix in one hand and Patrick tucked up beside her. Asking the question, what is going on here? One minute I'm counting out the pills to off myself, the next my life is turned inside out, and I keep wanting to laugh. The cave is filled with light, like someone took the roof

A certain woman had a vivid dream. In it she saw a man with

untidy long hair and bare feet sitting on a bench outside the

Post Office. A voice said to her that if she were to ask this man,

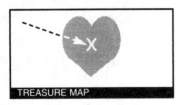

TREASURE MAP

he would give her something that

would make her rich forever. She

woke and shrugged the dream off. But the next day, while

walking through town, she saw the man from her dream sitting

on the bench outside the Post Office. Feeling somewhat foolish,

she approached the man and explained her dream. He listened,

off. How did it happen? How did I get from there to here?
She is remembering the mysterious courier package. So where
was that from? Don't they normally have a sender's address on
those things?

And then she is watching herself from above, with that
bottle of pills and the blackness over her. And she hears again her
question. 'Is there anyone out there?' Her fingers, then as now,
wrapped around that little man on the cross. Was that it? That
question, that gut-cry? Is this some kind of answer? From who?

The God question—that's a biggy. And if there were to be

and then reached into his rucksack. He produced an enormous

gold nugget, saying, 'I found this beside the river. Here, it's

yours if you want it.'

She gladly took the nugget. It was huge, sufficient to make

her wealthy for the rest of her life. But that night she could not

sleep, tossing and turning in her bed. At dawn she set out to

find the tramp, who was sleeping under a tree in the park.

She returned the nugget to him and said, 'Give me that wealth

that makes it possible for you to give this treasure away.'

a God thingy, why would it be interested in a case-hardened
suicidal hooker like me?

'Patrick, you and me, we've been through everything
together. You're the only one in the whole of the world who's
never let me down. Every night, after it's all over, we have the
bed to ourselves and we look after each other. We don't trust
anyone else, and that's how we've got through. But now I'm
scared, Patrick. There's weird stuff going down. I don't want to
lose control. What do you think, hairy one? Are we going to let
Vincent in? You'd like him, I know you would. I like him a lot.

I give what I was given...

I guess life itself is a gift. It's not something you can demand or organize for yourself. You just wake up one day and discover you've been given it. The only way to keep it fresh is to give it away. The more you give, the more flows in to take its place. But if you try to keep it, to hang on to it and keep it safe, it goes rotten on you. And the stink is awful.

WHOEVER WANTS TO SAVE THEIR LIFE WILL

But it's all so screwed up Patrick, all so terribly screwed up. If you're out there, you God-thingy, can you help me find a way through this?

#

For the past six weeks he has been keeping a journal. It grew out of the Buddhism thing, and something he read in one of the books. It's a patchy sort of attempt—half the time he forgets. But Vincent finds it helpful to write things down, to

JESUS OF NAZARETH

↕

LOSE IT.

→

try to make some sense out of the kaleidoscope. This morning it seems to be writing itself on the page.

The new person in my life is Marilyn. She flew in from another planet and has me locked in some kind of tractor beam. I can't do anything without thinking about her. I keep staring at the terminal at work, totally lost. How is it that someone can come into your life from the outside, and make such a mess of it in such a short space of time? Not that I mind—it's the sort of mess I've dreamed about. Relationships are so bloody complicated. There you are minding your own business when—without warning—this human

P A G E

127

Creating

Creating is not the same as making. You can make a bed, but you have to create a garden. Making is what manufacturers do. Creating is what poets and lovers do. You can make something without investing anything of yourself. Nothing was ever created, on the other hand, that didn't have a piece of the creator in it. Creation begins in the heart, whatever it may end up as. It is a work of love. Creation takes time.

It is the beginning of all spirituality.

In the beginning, there was **chaos**. And the **Spirit** hovered and brooded and made love to the **nothingness**, until the **Earth** was formed.

asteroid blazes through your atmosphere and totals your defensive screens.

Does this have anything to do with my search to find something true in life? I thought I was supposed to be loosening my attachment to life, but this seems to be moving in the opposite direction. Does spirituality have any meeting point with the love of another person?

I'm beginning to think I'm not really cut out for the ascetic life. Does that disqualify me? What about all the other people like me, who are so busy they don't know their arse from their elbow?

So how does GOD feel?

The most important part of creativity is love. If you want to create something that has life (and everything created has life), you first of all have to decide to give up some of your own life. Where else did you think the life was going to come from? It inevitably costs something to be a creator. You're hanging a bit of your life out there in the public domain. When people react to whatever it is you have made, they are reacting to you. So why would anyone create anything? It's a primal thing. When the seed of love burrows into your heart, and strikes roots there, it begins to grow upwards and outwards. Love is not love until it has expressed itself in some way.

Are we not good enough to be spiritual, because we are caught up in mundanity? That's a depressing thought.

And what about this God question? What sort of God would have made a world like this one? Is God a psychotic? And then there's the basic problem—how would you ever go about finding out whether there is a God or not? Where would you start looking? No use consulting religious people, they're all too certain about the truth. Where would I look for God? Maybe God is looking for me. Who knows? Too many questions, not enough pure pleasure.

Marilyn, Marilyn, Marilyn.

And God said: Let be...

The universe was made from love. That is its deepest secret. Because it has been created out of love, it calls to us. It summons us to be part of the ongoing adventure of creation. The universe woos us and lures us. It asks of us that we might give what is in us to give; that we join our creativity to the vast stream which is already flowing. None of us can ever discover who we are until we have begun to create. We are **created** and we are **creators**. It is our essence to draw from the deep well of imagination, and forge newness out of nothing. Work has made us into producers, but we know in some neglected part of us that we were made for more than this. We were made to be artists.

'Why are you so uptight about it? It's cosmic, that's what it is. It's meant to be, so why fight it?'

'It may be cosmic, Paula, but it's not simple. As soon as he finds out I'm on the game, it'll be bye bye Vincent.'

'There's a lot of negative energy there, Marilyn, but you may have a point. I suppose there's no way of keeping it secret?'

... and it was

'Yeah sure. Excuse me, Vincent, I'll be a bit late for dinner cos I'm busy screwing a client. You're welcome to come up later on, but I'll just have to change the sheets.'

'Okay, okay. You really need to get a massage, darling, your tension levels are way high. In the meantime, we've got to work out what you're going to do. Have you done the I Ching? I know a wonderful woman who'll read your skull—she's just marvellous, really she is.'

'Paula, do you think there's a God?'

And God saw that it was good...

Consciousness Realization Experiment

'Of course there's a God. What do you think I've been on about all these years? God is in everything and everything is in God. You are God, darling, if only you could see it and understand it.'

'No, I'm not God and I don't want to be God. If I was God, do you think I'd be turning tricks for a living? My life's a disaster area—if I'm God then there's no hope for any of us. I'm sick of all this bullshit, Paula. I want a God who is different from me, who is not me, who is somehow better than me.'

Some people think they're not very creative. That's because of one of two things. Either they haven't been loved enough, or else they haven't learned to love enough. Creating is a simple matter of opening the channel so that the tide can flow.

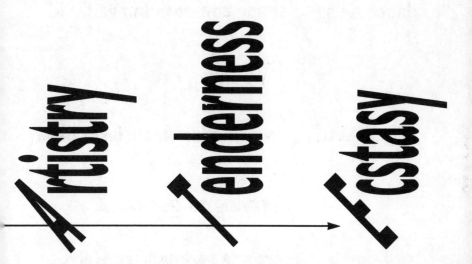

'Well, if that's the God you want, then that's the God you'll get.'

'That's no help to me at all. I don't want a God I've created, for Christ's sake. I'm talking about a real God who is alive separately from me. Someone I can talk to and who might think differently from me. Is that too much to ask for?'

'I don't have any problems with you following your own path, sweetie. That's the only way any of us progress.'

'But if there were to be a God like I'm talking about, then

paint write laugh draw sculpt cry act speak

There are things

dance design / shape compose image build

inside you

listen sketch grow \ sing jam transform believe

trying to get out...

sew nurture improvise serenade conceive

---

it would be important for all of us, can't you see? It would **matter.'**

'But what sort of God are you talking about? People have been making up their own versions for centuries. Do you want a God who tells people to kill little babies, or who supports wars, or who hates women? Half of the bigotry and violence of the whole human race has used the name of God. The whole idea of one universal God has outlived its usefulness. We're past the use-by date for that sort of God.'

'Maybe you're right. I just have this gut feeling that

Anyone who creates shares the life of God. If you experience the life of God, you will create. The only hard part is the sort of lives we settle for. It's very hard to fit your ⎯⎯⎯⎯⎯⎯⎯⎯⎯

into a

↓

Don't even try.

someone or something is out there, and I don't know who it is.' And there she goes, fingering that cross again.

#

Maybe she's got FTC. I thought failure to commit was the man's prerogative. She's been reserved all through dinner. Oh God, I'm so scared of losing her.

'Vincent?'

'Mmmm.'

'There's ah... there's something we need to talk about.'

Friendship

Shirley this is not going to be another one of those wanky definitions of friendship, is it? You know, A friend is... sort of stuff. Who the hell cares what a friend is if you can't find one? Last time I looked, no one was feeling bereft of definitions. It's people we're looking for. There's no checklist of qualities they have to have. Just someone who knows us and yet still loves us. That's a big ask.

'Only if you want to. I'm happy just to sit here and look at you. Sorry, this looks like something serious.' Looks a lot like the intro to the Dear John speech, truth be told.

'It's about me and what I do.'

'Yeah, I wondered when you were going to pluck up the courage to talk about it. Don't tell me, you work for the CIA, right? Sorry, sorry, I'll shut up.'

She is totally absorbed in the remains of her salad, scrutinizing it for something. Anything to avoid his eyes.

I knew this big guy. Fairly straight down the line sort of a person,
if you know what I mean. We didn't always see eye to eye.
I remember when I was doing a bit of anti-apartheid protesting,
some fairly heavy stuff. He objected to the tactics involved.
We had a bit of a discussion about it. It got fairly aggro;
I threatened to punch his lights out. Ambitious, really, seeing he
was twice my size. Later on, I got arrested during a demo.
By the time they released me from the cells, it was late at night.
Guess who was waiting for me? There with his car to give me
a ride home. The big guy. He's a friend of mine.

'There's no easy way of saying this. I'm a prostitute.
I sleep with men for my living. It's a business. I'm very
professional.'

Time and silence have this thing they do together.
They make a chasm that has no bottom to it. And there you
are, standing right on the edge of it. Aware that at any moment
you may be falling and falling and falling, with no hope of
recovery. At the moment they are at either side of it, each
consumed by their private terror. She looks up at last from
her salad. Vincent is crying. The tears are streaming down

I want someone to be **with** me when everything is going down. I don't care in the end if they're cool or smart or cute or strong. Just so long as when I get out the other side, they're still with me. Don't need to say anything,

Beware of friends with no r s.

to fix anything, to buy anything, to do anything. But they do need to be something. And that something is **there**.

The one thing more important than finding a friend is **being** a friend. When's the last time you sat down and were thankful for your friends? Thought about them; held them in the warmth of your imagination? Maybe dreamed up one simple thing you could do to express your friendship—

his cheeks, and he is biting his lip to stop himself sobbing.

'I'm sorry. I didn't mean to deceive you. I'm sorry, Vincent, I'm sorry.'

He can't speak. He wants to, but nothing is working. He is looking at her, at her beautiful face, at her eyes, at the slight hardness round her mouth. And weeping and weeping. She reaches a hand across to hold his. She is beyond tears, empty and bleak and barren. Vincent is mumbling something, but is incoherent through the pain. And then he begins to repeat it again and again.

The best mirror is an old friend

to let them know that you were there with them?

Write something; say something; send something; make something; do something. Friendship is like soil—if you don't feed it now and again, then you can't keep coming back and expecting there'll be a harvest.

Do it now!

'I love you, I love you, I love you, I love you...'

This is the worst thing she has ever heard in her life. She wants to scream, to break something, to tip over the table in rage. Instead some continental shelf rips loose within her. She begins gulping and moaning, a terrible agonizing cry from another place. And the tears are flowing. They grip each other's hands, and lean their foreheads together. The tears are flowing into the abyss, and there is no end to them.

#

No <u>one</u> has greater love than this;

that they lay down their life for

their friends.

JESUS OF NAZARETH

I don't remember anything about how we got back here, he is thinking. Here they are, in Marilyn's flat. He is holding her, comforting her. She has hardly stopped crying since the café.

He says nothing. Sometimes he is tempted to, but every thought seems trivial against the sheer size of the grief. And so he sits on the couch, holding her while she sobs. He has his own confusion and pain, but by some great effort of will has pushed the future to one side. Which leaves only the present.

The neon sign from across the road washes the room with

I get by with a little help from my friends...

Now who said that?

Friendship is a way of living that goes right to the heart of existence. When we have learned to be friends to ourselves and friends to each other, then we can become friends of the planet, friends of the poor, friends of the birds and animals, friends of the forests and seas. And both before that and after it and during it and because of it; we can be friends of God.

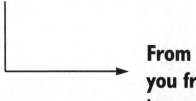

From now on I call you friends...
Jesus of Nazareth (again)

red at regular intervals. He is aware of something shining in the light. It is the cross which Marilyn wears around her neck. He cradles it in his palm and examines it. A man nailed to a cross, naked and vulnerable. I know what that feels like. To be stretched out on the grid of reality and fixed there, so that there's no escape.

The heaving has subsided, and Vincent sees that she has fallen asleep. Tenderly, he lays her out on the couch, and finds a blanket from the bedroom to cover her. He kneels there, and strokes her face as she sleeps. All the hardness is gone from her

```
LOVELOVELOVELOVELOVELOVE     LOVELOVELOVELOVELOVE          LOVELO
LOVELOVELOVELOVELOVELOVE     LOVELOVELOVELOVELOVELO        LOVELO
LOVELOVELOVELOVELOVELOVE     LOVELOVE        LOVELOVEL     LOVELO
LOVELOVE                     LOVELOVE           LOVELOVE   LOVELO
LOVELOVE                     LOVELOVE             LOVELOV  LOVELO
LOVELOVE                     LOVELOVE          LOVELOVE    LOVELO
LOVELOVELOVELOVELOVELOVE     LOVELOVE        ELOVELOVE     LOVELO
LOVELOVELOVELOVELOVELOVE     LOVELOVELOVELOVELOVELO        LOVELO
LOVELOVE                     LOVELOVELOVELOVE              LOVELO
LOVELOVE                     LOVELOVE    LOVELOVE          LOVELO
LOVELOVE                     LOVELOVE      LOVELOVE        LOVELO
LOVELOVE                     LOVELOVE        LOVELOVE      LOVELO
LOVELOVE                     LOVELOVE          LOVELOVE    LOVELO
LOVELOVE                     LOVELOVE            LOVELOVE   LOVELO
LOVELOVE                     LOVELOVE              LOVELOVE LOVELO
LOVELOVE                     LOVELOVE              LOVELOVE LOVELO
LOVELOVE                     LOVELOVE             LOVELOVE  LOVELO
LOVELOVE                     LOVELOVE            LOVELOVE   LOVELO
```

If the enemy of my enemy is my friend,

The sting of suffering is loneliness.
You can survive an enormous amount
of pain if you don't have to do it alone.
To have a warm hand to hang on to,
and a familiar voice in your ear; that's
enough to give you some strength for
another day.

in sleep, and she is innocent. After a time he stumbles through to the bedroom, and is lost in softness and oblivion.

The unfamiliar light wakes her early. There is a great psychic bruise which lurks beneath consciousness. The details take some time to arrange themselves. She stumbles through to the bedroom and is relieved to see him there. She lifts his hair back from his face, and kisses his temple. He squirms but does not wake. She makes coffee in the kitchen, and carries the two

```
OVELOVELOVELOVELOVELOVE     LOVELOVELOVELOV        LOVELOVE    LOVELOVELOVELOV
OVELOVELOVELOVELOVELOVE     LOVELOVELOVELOVE       LOVELOVE    LOVELOVELOVELOVELOV
OVELOVELOVELOVELOVELOVE     LOVELOVE LOVELOVE      LOVELOVE    LOVELOVE    LOVELOVE
OVELOVE                     LOVELOVE  LOVELOVE     LOVELOVE    LOVELOVE      LOVELOVE
OVELOVE                     LOVELOVE  LOVELOVE     LOVELOVE    LOVELOVE       LOVELOVE
OVELOVE                     LOVELOVE   LOVELOVE    LOVELOVE    LOVELOVE        LOVELOVE
OVELOVELOVELOVELOVELOVE     LOVELOVE   LOVELOVE    LOVELOVE    LOVELOVE        LOVELOVE
OVELOVELOVELOVELOVELOVE     LOVELOVE    LOVELOVE   LOVELOVE    LOVELOVE        LOVELOVE
OVELOVE                     LOVELOVE     LOVELOVE  LOVELOVE    LOVELOVE        LOVELOVE
OVELOVE                     LOVELOVE      LOVELOVE LOVELOVE    LOVELOVE        LOVELOVE
OVELOVE                     LOVELOVE       LOVELOVELOVELOVE    LOVELOVE        LOVELOVE
OVELOVE                     LOVELOVE        LOVELOVEOVELOVE    LOVELOVE        LOVELOVE
OVELOVE                     LOVELOVE         LOVELOVLOVELOVE   LOVELOVE        LOVELOVE
OVELOVE                     LOVELOVE          LOVELOVELOVELO   LOVELOVE        LOVELOVE
OVELOVE                     LOVELOVE           LOVELOVELOVEV   LOVELOVE        LOVELOVE
OVELOVE                     LOVELOVE            LOVELOVELOVEL  LOVELOVE        LOVELOVE
OVELOVELOVELOVELOVE         LOVELOVE             LOVELOVELOLO LOVELOVE    LOVELOVELO
OVELOVELOVELOVELOVE         LOVELOVE              LOVELOVELOV LOVELOVELOVELOVELOVELOVE
OVELOVELOVELOVELOVELOVE     LOVELOVE               LOVELOVELOV LOVELOVELOVELOVE
```

why isn't the friend of my friend my enemy?

mugs through to the bedroom. With trepidation she massages his shoulder, and watches him break the surface. He looks at her and smiles, and reaches up to kiss her. The coffee grows cold.

They lie side by side, naked.

    'Where do we go from here?' she asks.

    'I've been thinking about that.'

    'When?'

Birth and Dying

Everything starts with a beginning. Except for when it starts with an ending. Or ends in a birth. There's some sort of connection here.

Between beginnings and endings. Perhaps they're closer together than you might think.

I was calm and at peace. There seemed to be a balance between things. I felt very content and complete, as if I had reached some new level of fullness. It hit me quite suddenly. A sense of collapse; a terrible shuddering shock which gripped my body like the talons of a hawk. And then I knew I was moving, drifting, and there was nothing at all I could do about it. It was time to leave. I found myself in a long dark tunnel, being propelled along it. It was frightening. And then, at the end of the tunnel—a light. It grew brighter and brighter, until suddenly I emerged from the darkness and there was nothing but light, light, light...

'Last night, you little bundle of insecurities.'

'And?'

'Let me tell you one of my stories. My father had an old pair of boots that were his favourites. He gave them a fair old hiding, and they eventually cracked just behind the toe. Well, you'll be needing a new pair of boots, says Mum. But Dad says he's not so sure about that. So he takes his old boots down to the cobblers to see what they can do. No problem, the cobbler says, we'll revamp them. What's that involve, my father wants to know. We unpick the stitching around here, he shows him, and

What is this story? An account of a birth or a death? There's no way of knowing. The death we fear may be the birth we seek.

Both birth and death are passive—we have very little control over them. Maybe that's why we're scared. But they are as natural as

breathing. In fact, maybe that's what birth and death are all about—the inhaling and exhaling of the universe.

B i r

D e a

we fit a new vamp in and sew them up again. You see, the vamp is the part that wears out. There's nothing wrong with the rest of the boot. That's what we mean by revamping. So he leaves them there, and a couple of days later he comes home wearing his favourite boots, good as new. Mum was furious.'

'Now let me guess where I fit in this story. Am I the vamp or an old boot?'

'The point is, you bare-breasted literalist, that there is often a new way forward. We need to look at what we've got, and see what needs to be revamped to get us going again.'

This set down
This: were we led all that way for
Birth or Death? There was a Birth,
    certainly,
We had evidence and no doubt.
I had seen birth and death,
But had thought they were different...

T.S. ELIOT, FROM 'JOURNEY OF THE MAGI'

To be there, when life comes to birth or reaches death, is to be in the presence of a sacred mystery. It is like standing at the doors of being, and feeling the winds of life breezing through. Sometimes it is messy; always it is real. Like finally touching solid ground after floating in the sea for days on end.

From the beginning of our living, we are dying, and our dying is the way to life. Once you have understood this, there is not much left to understand.

'This is the most confusing time in my entire life. I don't know which way is up anymore.'

'Tell me about it.'

It all seemed so simple that they wondered what the problem had been. Marilyn's double bed fitted Vincent's bedroom with about six inches to spare either side. He refused to let go of his yellow lounge chair and she insisted on bringing her coffee table. He would never have been the one to suggest she stop,

Birth and death are to be celebrated, not ignored. We have developed a morbid fear of processes which are both inevitable and natural. Death is only an enemy to those who fear it. Birth is only of value to those who embrace it. In all of our daily decisions, in all of our greetings and partings, in all of our loving and ceasing to love, in all of our taking up and our laying down, there is the rhythm of birth and death. The task of living is the learning of dying, so that we might be born again.

> The pain of giving up is the pain of death, but death of the old is birth of the new. The pain of death is the pain of birth, and the pain of birth is the pain of death.
>
> **M. Scott Peck, The Road Less Travelled**

and she would not have accepted it if it had have come from him. Paula helped her redistribute her clients, and Marilyn couldn't think of one of them she would miss. It would be tight for a while on Vincent's money, but she would find some sort of work. Although he felt slightly claustrophobic, the whole process happened so quickly it was like riding some huge wave. You don't get to think about it until it's gone.

The cat quickly adjusted to Marilyn. She wanted to name it, but Vincent feared domestication. They both liked to cook, when they weren't too tired. Most of all they liked to go walking

Once you're dead, you're made for life.

JIMI HENDRIX

There's a time for every purpose under heaven— a time for **BIRTH** and a time for **DEATH**.

ECCLESIASTES

in the park after Vincent had got home from work, to ease their way into the evening. There was always something to talk about.

#

Thus it was that Marilyn's dreams took them both by surprise. She would wake up crying in the middle of the night, and Vincent would need to hold both her and Patrick until she slept again. He didn't pry, but one night she started to talk, unprompted.

The trick in life is knowing which is which. There's a time for springing forth in birth and a time for letting go in death. The pain of death is always relinquishment. That's why it's helpful to practise letting go before it's all gone.

Dying well is just like anything else... it takes practice.

The more you hang on to life, the tighter you clench it in your fists, the more fiercely you defend it and seek to possess it, the more quickly it runs away through your fingers. The secret of birth is the same as the secret of death:

Let Go!

'I'm always somewhere beautiful, either alone or with you. Tonight it was in a clearing in the forest, just at dusk. And then he turns up. My father. He stands there and watches, sometimes he laughs. It's like a giant shadow falling across a sunny day. I know what's going to happen, and I can't stop it. Then he's on me, pawing away at me. I can feel the weight of him on top of me, and smell his breath. That's when I wake up, and I have trouble making it all go away.'

'Have you ever talked to anyone about it?'

'Only Paula. Her father was the same—that's how we

Let Go!

Relax into it, breathe deeply, have someone to hold your hand. Above all, stop fighting against it. The whole of our life we are dying—in every parting, in every disappointment, in every loss, in every transition, we are learning how to die. The only mistake is to seek to protect ourselves from it.

became friends, really—we picked up each other's signals. It's not something you want to talk about with many people.'

'Is he still alive?'

'No, he died two years ago. Luckily I had shifted by then. It saved me a trip to go and spit on his grave. The bastard never thought of anyone except himself. I used to watch other girls with their fathers, and wonder if the same thing was happening to them. That's the worst part of it really. You don't know if it's normal or not. And when I figured out it was wrong, I thought it was my fault. He told me it was my fault,

born

that I shouldn't arouse him like that. I've wondered a million times why it had to happen to me. But there's no answers.'

'I love you, Marilyn.'

He wraps her up and holds her, blowing and whispering in her ear.

It's late in the evening when the phone rings. Vincent is writing in his journal. Marilyn is putting the new photos in her album. She's closest to the phone. It's Paula.

die

once?

'Oh God, Marilyn, I just had the strangest experience, and I have to talk to someone. You're not in bed, are you?'

'No, no; we're just kicking back. What's happened?'

'Well, I've been reading that creative visualization book, you know the one I told you about. I thought I'd try one of the exercises. You had to get your breathing organized, and then imagine yourself in a beautiful place. Everything was alright—I was picturing myself sitting beside a river with my feet in the water, feeling really peaceful, thinking of nothing in particular. And then I gradually became aware that there was someone beside me.'

Subversion

It's like there's all these people playing a board game. Each of them has a part to play, and a little counter thingy that they move round the squares on the board. They all understand the rules of the game, and they all play by them. There's winners and losers. But when you pull out of the game and look over their shoulders for a while, you realize that the entire game is crap. It doesn't matter who wins, because it's just a game. And so you set out to ruin the game. You decide not to play by the rules anymore. Why? Because life is too important to be playing games that have no meaning. So you spoil the game. You have become a subversive.

'Freaky.'

'It was a bit, but she wasn't frightening. She was incredibly beautiful, like she was glowing or something. Wearing all white, and I don't know, serene I guess would be the word for it. She looked at me and there was so much love in her eyes that I could hardly bear it. I mean it wasn't a sexual thing or anything, but it almost could have been. So I go, 'What do you want?' And she goes, 'I've got a message for you.' 'From who? I want to know. 'From the maker of dreams,' she says. 'What is it?' I ask her. Then she's quiet for a few moments, just looking

If the SYSTEM hates you, you will understand that it hated me before it hated you. If you belonged in the SYSTEM, the SYSTEM would welcome you as its own. Because you don't belong to the SYSTEM, but I have called you out of it—therefore the SYSTEM hates you.

JESUS TALKS TO HIS FRIENDS

at me. And it's like she can see right to the bottom of my soul, you know, like there's nothing hidden from her. 'Paula,' she says. She called me by name, I can still hear the way she said it. 'Paula, you need to decide which side you're on. Light and darkness, good and evil, life and death. I've been waiting for you, and I always will. But only you can make the choice.' And then she reaches over and touches me on the forehead, and I fall flat on my back. I can hear music playing, and I feel so peaceful, like I've never felt in my life before. It was so good, Marilyn.'

```
Subversive's Shopping List


   Blank business cards    ✓
      Water pistol         ✓
      Vinyl records        ✓
   A broken television     ✓
   Map of the universe     ✓
      Play money           ✓
   3 false noses           ✓
   A book of dreams        ✓
 1 clock with no hands     ✓
      Brain floss          ✓
   Reason for living       ✓
      Other stuff          ✓
```

'Was that it?'

'Next thing I knew, I was waking up on the carpet in my room, stretched flat out. I hadn't been asleep, I don't think. I just lay there for a long time, and then I got up and had to ring you to tell you about it. What's it mean, do you think?'

'I don't know. It sounds like a visit from an angel or something.'

'Oh, Marilyn, that's exactly what I thought. Either an

Subversion is all about overlapping worlds, parallel universes, intersecting realities. A subversive looks the same as everyone else. Eats food, drinks water, breathes air. Some of them even catch buses and hold jobs. It's easy to mistake them for being **normal.** But the fact is that they're somewhere else altogether. Present, but living out of some alternative dream.

Subversion is more fun than six frogs in a bowl. The main task of the subversive is to disrupt games which are unworthy of life. Break them up like smashing the ice on the top of a puddle. The people who are running the games tend not to be appreciative of the subversive's contribution. After all, their games are ways of holding things together in the face of life. You have to keep things tidy. We need some control. Where would we all be if everyone took your attitude? It's for their own good. They get a lot out of our games.

Don't
eat what you can't stomach

angel or an alien. It's just so **exciting**. To think someone would have a message for me.'

'What do you make of the message?'

'I guess I need to make some choices, but I'm not sure exactly what they are. One thing I know—the way I was feeling after she touched me, I don't ever want to lose that. I'm going down to Pathways Books tomorrow, to get everything they've got on angels.'

'Let me know if you figure it out.'

Top Ten Subversive Lines...

1. I have enough money, thanks all the same.

2. What are you passionate about?

I don't have enough time to get busy. **3.**

Have you ever really stopped and asked yourself why you do what you do? **4.**

If all your problems were solved, what would you worry about?

5.

#

The reason I haven't written much of any depth lately is because there's been nothing to say. I guess I've been drifting along, floating on the surface and enjoying it. Marilyn has brought so many good things into my life. She's a funny mixture of tough and fragile. I wonder what chance we've got together. Last night we talked about all sorts of things. Started off talking about angels, because Paula had had some sort of vision. Then we got on to death, and whether

6.

**My doctor has told me I'm dying—
I only have 60 years left.**

7.

**Moderation in all things,
including moderation.**

8.

**What has that person to gain by
teaching you that?**

9.

Who's making the decisions?

10. → **What lies have you told or lived lately?**

it was just an end, or whether there was something beyond it.
Neither of us can accept that this is all there is. It would just be too
depressing beyond words. But what then? Reincarnation? The
seemingly endless cycle of trying to make up for past stuff-ups,
scrambling up the spiritual scaffold? Seems too much like hard work
to me, which I've never been keen on. A sort of cosmic version of
economic rationalism. The Zen thing? Instant enlightenment? That
has something going for it, but how do you find the trigger? And it
still doesn't answer the death issue. Though maybe it would if it
happened.

What you see is what you get.

You can't have your cake and eat it too.

You'll come right once you grow up and settle down.

I used to feel that when I was your age.

A bird in the hand is worth two in the bush.

CRAP Always take clean underwear—
you don't know what might happen.

Respect your betters.

Don't eat with your mouth full.

Look after your pennies and the pounds will take
care of themselves.

It's rude to stare.

Keep off.

Marilyn raised the one-hit scenario. That this life is the only one we get, and that somehow determines what happens to us beyond death. I wanted to know how you could have that without all the heaven and hell stuff that seems to go along with it. She had no answers, but thought it tied in somehow with Paula's vision. It would certainly concentrate your attention if you thought this life was the only one you got.

But how fair would it be? What chance has a kid who dies of starvation at the age of twelve somewhere in the Sudan? For me it raises this God question again. If there were a God, what sort of God

version

sub

Within the skin of reality there
is another way of being. Largely
undiscovered, it reeks of life. Those
who have found it can never again be
satisfied with mere existence. They
become hungry for what they have
tasted, and refuse to succumb to the
pressures of normalcy.

would he/she/it be? Why would God be lurking around in the
shadows, instead of saying to us, this is who I am and this is how
things are supposed to be?

I guess I just get on with things and live like there is no God.
But if there is one, it would be nice to know. Where do these people
get off with all their certainty? Must be a good feeling to think
you've got the universe sewn up, and the truth for your personal
possession. As for me and mine, we just make do with what scraps
we can scab from experience.

Never be con- formed to the System

be trans- formed from the inside.

PAUL THE SUBVERSIVE

She lies there rigid. The sheet is pasted to her body with sweat. It is so strong that she is scared to open her eyes in case it should turn out to be real. She churns through the dream, trying to get enough distance to make sense of it.

It had been him again, of course, coming through to her bedroom in the early hours of the morning. The sound of the door handle creaking. She would pretend to be asleep, but he knew. He was on top of her, and there was the terrible burning

I laughed

Laughing may just be the greatest spiritual resource available to us, occupying as it does the wetlands between despair and insanity. In our laughing we give voice to the entire tragedy and joy of human survival in the warzone of life. Perhaps it is laughter which is the image of God within us.

It would be possible to think that humour is all about jokes and slapstick comedy. I find most comedians about as funny as the tax department. There

pain like being stabbed. Marilyn was away in her dreamworld that she used to escape to, talking to Patrick. There was the heavy thrusting, the rancid smell of him, his controlled breathing.

And then suddenly Patrick had disappeared, and there was someone else there. It was that man on the cross. He was naked and bleeding. They had him stretched out on the ground, on top of the cross. They were leaning over him, banging bloody great spikes through his wrists. He looked at Marilyn, he could see her watching. He mumbled something,

The difference between sex and death is that with death you can do it alone and no one is going to make fun of you.

WOODY ALLEN

is an air of quiet desperation in the way they strain to make us laugh—as if we had made a spectator sport out of watching a man trying to overcome his constipation. Shallow laughter leaves you with sore face muscles and an odd sensation at the back of your head, but little else.

Humour is the result of suffering. It grows among people whose life is so unredeemably shattered that they need a means of stepping outside of it for a time. The capacity to laugh deeply comes from the dark mills of pain, where souls are churned and crushed.

till I cried...

but she couldn't quite catch it. Something like 'I love you.' There was the terrible ringing sound of the steel hammer on the top of the spike, and the corresponding thud as it drove more deeply through flesh and wood-fibre.

The two worlds merged. Every time her father thrust hard into her, there was a corresponding blow with the hammer. There was some connection between the two—they were part of the same thing. And the man on the cross was looking at her, and he knew her, and he understood what was happening, and he was crying not with his pain but with hers. The blows and the

It only hurts when I Laugh...

LAugh...

Aaaaaaah

Humour is a form of protest. It is an alternative to suicide. Laughter reaches out toward the future and the goodness of life, even when there is none. It ridicules the self-importance of existence, puts it into perspective. The best of humour has an edge of self-mockery about it. It cuts through the bullshit and relieves the unrelenting seriousness of daily existence. The funniest people are also the saddest people. They see things as they really are, and that is why they laugh.

thrusts speeded up and intensified. Bang. Thrust. Bang. Thrust.

'Oh Jesus,' cried her father.

Oh Jesus.

\#

They walk through the park together, arm in arm. She is eating an ice-cream, which Vincent occasionally takes a lick at. They sit on a bench at the edge of the fish-pond, and watch the bloated goldfish glide along. Vincent is preoccupied with a sub-routine

HAVE YOU HEARD THE COSMIC JOKE?

Sexual and toilet humour is a revolutionary tool. That's why the poorest people love it and the richest people hate it. Subversives use it to puncture pretension. The distressing fact is, that no matter how famous or wealthy or intelligent a person is, they are burdened with certain bodily functions which are shared with the mass of humanity. It does no harm to remind people of this from time to time; to laugh at our embodied existence.

---

he's been trying to put together in his spare time at work.

'Will we get old and tired?' Marilyn asks.

'Too late.'

'Seriously. Do you think it will get harder to love each other? That one day we'll find that we've run out of things to talk about, and spend all our time fuming over the way the toilet roll's been hung?'

'I've told you, there's only one way to hang a toilet roll. What's to argue about it?'

Ancient Rule of Thumb:
It is better to be pissed off
than to be pissed on.

in the midst
of the

pain

Laugh Laugh Laugh

hold on

'I'm scared, Vincent. You spend your life organizing things so that no one can get on the inside. And then you wake up to find that some skinny poser has got past your defences. It's all so predictable, isn't it? When's the last time you heard of a relationship that lasted, I mean like more than ten years? Then I think, well what's the point of getting involved if you're just going to have to get hurt and find ways of hating each other? Except I can't help myself. So I end up living with the love and the pain at the same time, like some neurotic sicko.'

The greatest egotism is to take yourself too seriously. I'm sure not even God is guilty of that. Give me another explanation for giraffes. Survival in Millennium Three depends on being willing and able to stand far enough away from your life to laugh at yourself.

The resurrection is a joke...

You either get it or you don't. No explanations.

The truth about the death of Jimi Hendrix: it wasn't his own vomit!
GRAFFITI

'You think it's that inevitable? That we won't last?'

'I'm too scared to think anything else. Then I'd get my hopes up, and I'd be a real goner.'

'So what do we do? Try and keep our risks to a minimum? Hold back something for the sake of the future? I don't think I know how to do that.'

'Neither of us do. That's why we're such a couple of losers. Don't you wish there was something solid and constant to hold on to?'

If we are going to live together we will need to learn to laugh together. But in order to laugh together, we must cry together. You can see why people prefer to stay on their own.

Madness
is simply forgetting what it is you're laughing about...

Without humour we are all in danger of losing our way. It is the gift of the angels, but even they have become jealous of the way we have developed it. We are human; let us laugh till the cows come home.

'I guess. For the meantime I'm just happy to hang on to you.'
'Fool,' she says, kissing him.

The light at either end of the day is mysterious. Here in the early morning it is washing Marilyn's skin with a sort of tawny gold. Vincent is jacked up on one arm, watching her. The slow waves of breath the only sign of life. He has the time to take in all the details. Imperfections in the texture of her skin. The thick hair under her armpit. A small scar on the back of her

Nurturing

Everything that is tender needs a little protection as it grows. Looking after the fragile and vulnerable is called nurturing. There's bits of me as old and hard and woody as ancient vines, but there's also bits that are fresh and green and just starting out. I need some nurture from time to time.

The way that any of us learn to nurture is by being nurtured ourselves. If you didn't get it at your mother's breast, then you're going to spend the rest of your life looking for it. A lot of men continue looking for it even when they've had it! But the deepest nurture is nurture of yourself. You need to tend your soul, to cosset it and shelter it and feed it, so that it may grow. As you learn how to care for yourself, it may be that you can extend that care to the nurturing of others.

The force that

through the green

fuse drives the flower

Drives my green age

DYLAN THOMAS

---

neck which she got in a car accident. To observe her body is not to know her. This is the same body that was accessible to her clients, the same body that might be handled one day by a funeral director. It is Marilyn, but less than Marilyn. It's only when you know who she is that you can really see her body in the right way.

He is in love, whatever that means in these times. For the moment it means that as he lies there watching her, he is overwhelmed with gratitude. A deep unsolicited thankfulness which rises from some hidden place within. Here and now

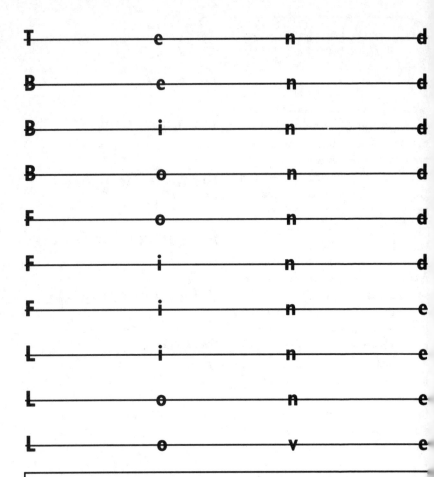

there is a sense that nothing else is necessary, that the feeling of well-being is sufficient unto itself. Except for the overwhelming desire to say thank you. But to whom? Well, even if there's no one listening, even if this is all that there is, thank you anyway.

There was a time when he was around eight years old, full of swagger and certainty. The family dog had just died. An ageing mongrel called Pal, with a greying snout. He had reached the stage where he wasn't up to much anymore, apart from

This old earth is getting tired of us. We have plundered and abused and strip-mined, and left our mess behind to poison the soil. We have treated our environment as if it were some sort of supply store-cum-

Nurture

It is time to change; to cease abusing and begin nurturing. We have begun to understand almost too late that we are in relationship with the earth; that we have a responsibility to tend and husband the gift of this planet. It is not up to somebody else to fix things. You and I need to change the way we live.

Nature

rubbish dump. For aeons the earth has tolerated us, soaking up our violence like a battered woman who still loves her abuser. But now there is no capacity left to absorb any more.

Mature

Manure

toxifying the atmosphere with the exhaust from a failed digestive system. His little sister Katie doted on the dog. Vincent had lost interest when Pal stopped running and jumping.

Anyway, Katie insisted on a funeral. So there they all were, gathered round a hole in the backyard that was only a little bigger than Pal's remains. Vincent remembered that they had to tuck his tail in and bend his nose down to make him fit. They decided to each tell a story about Pal to celebrate him. Vincent told them about Pal and the lunch box. The two of them had

SO GOD LED THEM INTO THE GARDEN OF EDEN TO TEND IT AND TO NURTURE IT

been on an adventure together, fishing. He had baited up a hook and dropped his line over the side of a small bridge into the river below. Pal was happy checking out the history of the area with his nose. There may not have been any fish in the river. Vincent was dreaming, miles away, when he nudged his lunchbox with his foot and it fell into the river.

You couldn't get down to the water easily because the banks were steep. Seeing his lunch float away, Vincent used a range of commands to get Pal to go and fetch it. But Pal just stood there looking bemused and wagging his tail. So Vincent

A bruised reed he will not break, and a dimly burning wick he will not quench...

Look after everything that has life. Learn to be gentle from the inside out. Practise tenderness as a way of life. Grow something that you can have a relationship with, even if it's only mould on the bathroom wall. Remember that anything not yet fully formed is vulnerable, and easily damaged.

picked him up, carried him to the handrail of the bridge, and threw him into the water. This did not produce the desired result. Pal swam the opposite direction to the lunchbox, and tried to get up on the bank. It was too sleep and slippery, and he kept falling back into the water. Eventually Vincent had to tie some fishing line to his belt and the bridge, and ease his way down to rescue the dog. When they got back up to the bridge, Pal expressed his gratitude by shaking himself all over Vincent. That was Pal.

When they had all finished their stories, and Katie was

Growing to maturity on the planet brings responsibilities, whether we want them or not. Let us harbour the life that is within us.

crying, their father cast around for some final word to sum things up. He was obviously out of his depth in this role. Eventually he said something about meeting Pal again in heaven. Probably to make Katie feel better, Vincent suspected.

The others went inside, and Vincent and his father stayed behind to fill in the hole.

'You know what you said about Pal in heaven?'

'Mmmm.'

How to Grow Things

Make space for them to grow.

✳

Feed them regularly with what they need.

✳

Protect them against anything that would harm.

✳

Chop off the dead bits.

✳

Watch them.

✳

Talk to them.

✳

Sing to them.

✳

Set them free to grow their own.

'Well, that's not true, is it? We're putting him in this hole and he's going to rot away until there's only his bones left. So how can he be somewhere else at the same time?'

'Was Pal only his bones?'

'No, he had fur and teeth and lots of fat.'

'What will happen to all that?'

'Most of it will rot away and turn into dirt or something.'

'So where will Pal be?'

'All over the place, I guess.'

Nurture

'Is that how you'll think about Pal? Bits of stuff all over the place?'

'Nah.'

'How then?'

'I'll think about him like he was when we used to go fishing, or when he would play with me in the backyard.'

'So where will Pal be for you?'

'In my memory, I guess.'

'Well maybe heaven is God's memory.'

'Can we go inside now? I'm hungry.'

I'm wired to the world and it feels good. Out there trucking through the tundra of cyberia. Making connections, you know what I mean? Sparking like a synapse, piping the neural network of the new culture.

Log in, Lock on, Link up.

Link up.Link up.Link up.Link up.Link up.Link up.

#

It was the night of Paula's birthday. Vincent had cooked, and they got through a quantity of wine. Paula was looking radiant. Marilyn hadn't ever seen her so happy. She wanted to know why.

'I've made a lot of changes.'

'Like what? Your knickers?'

'Let's see now. I'm off the game, I've got a job, I'm not doing any drugs, I'm eating properly and I don't hate myself anymore.'

Tele-vision means to see

REDWEIRDWIREDWEIRDWIREDWEIRDWIREDWEI

'Paula! What happened? You become a frigging Hare Krishna or something?'

'I haven't become anything. You know the angel thingy I told you about? Well, I decided to adopt her as my spiritual guide. All sorts of things have been happening since then.'

'Tell us, tell us.'

'It's pretty heavy stuff. I'd rather talk about it when I'm partially sober. Tonight I just want to enjoy.'

'Fair enough. But don't think we're going to forget about

Technosurfing has twice as much buzz as astral travelling, and you can stay awake. I'm hanging ten on my silicon deck, catching the edge of the techno-tsunami.

WEIRDWIREDWEIRDWIREDWIREDWEIRDWIREDWEIR

far away...

it. You don't get away with becoming an instant saint without having to justify yourself to us, you know.'

'We really would like to hear about it,' Vincent added from the kitchen, where he was opening another bottle.

#

In the event they never did. Paula was found two days later in her flat by the neighbour who kept a key for emergencies. She was naked, her body dappled with bruises. The cord with which she had been strangled was still around her neck. She had been

World Wired Web

I'm going out from myself.
Extending my psyche into cyberspace.
Seeing what it might rub up against.
The universe is falling open before me,
peeling back under the touch of my
fingers. I'm transcending my limits;
reaching out beyond the confines
of space and time.
I'm a button-punching,
system-cracking,
mouse-clicking,
web-crawling,
remote-waving,
cyber-surfing
son of a gun.

All reality

raped, the police deduced, though it was so obvious that the neighbour recognized that much straight away. The detective who interviewed Marilyn tried to appear keen, but once it had been established what Paula had done for a living, you could see his eyelids drop.

The funeral was miserable. Paula's mother was vaguely Anglican, so the undertaker arranged a supply priest, and the service took place in the funeral parlour. The chapel was dark,

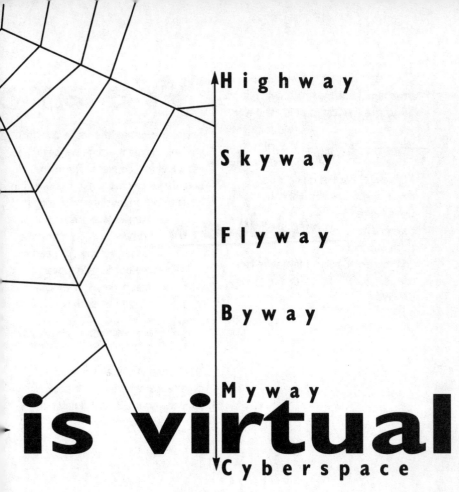

Highway

Skyway

Flyway

Byway

Myway

is virtual

Cyberspace

and every visible wooden surface was varnished. It smelled of mothballs. The priest read from a book. He said nothing of Paula apart from her name, and he even got that wrong at one point. The strange words, full of thees and thous, seemed to Marilyn an ancient incantation. She understood none of it, growing angrier and angrier as the farce went on. She wanted to get up and shout 'Stop! This is my friend Paula you're talking about.' But she didn't, unsure of the consequences.

Afterwards, they all filed out past the bloodless priest, but Marilyn stayed behind.

Plug in,

The future is coming down a tube in my room. I don't want to switch it off. Of course I'm scared of it. Whoever stood upright in a gale without being frightened? But I'm riding it out. I'm surfing the edges while the wave keeps rolling. The air is fresh out there,

Push on,

and there's no rules. Maybe we can reinvent ourselves. Or find out who we are.

We are

This is our planet, the space on which we live. Maybe it is time we began to get a feel for the place. There are no boundaries any more. No borders. No limits to our friendships or sharing of stories. We are strolling in cyberspace, breathing the ether, getting our bearings. When the borders disappear, who does that make us? If we can think together, if the earth is our

Phase out.

playground, if virtuality is valid experience, where does it take us? Only the courageous will find out. Don't miss the train.

'I'll see you outside,' she said to Vincent.

Alone in the chapel with the coffin, she leaned on the lid and wept.

'You bitch,' she said. 'You total bitch. Who said you could run out on me without permission? Who bloody told you you could go, huh? I'm really pissed off at you now, Paula. Really, really pissed off. You wait till I get hold of you.'

When the next contraction of grief had passed, she found herself draped across the top of the coffin.

connected...

You will know the truth, and the truth will set you

→ *free...*

'Paula, Paula, Paula. Who did this to you, baby? Who would do this to you? Why did they hurt you? Why didn't someone stop it, Paula? Why is it allowed to go on like this?'

There was no answer.

\#

Paula is dead. I can't quite get my head around it. Marilyn is devastated. I have just put her to bed with a hot toddy. I can't say that I knew Paula very well, but I liked her a lot. She was kind of goofy, a sucker for everything that came along. She had

Story

The world is multi-sto-ried

We all have our stories to tell. They may not have happened, but they are all true. I am sick of lectures/theories/principles/dogmas/regulations/explanations. I want to hear stories. I want to know the time and place, the smell of the air, the colour of the trees, the drift of the conversation. So don't tell me what you believe or how you think. Tell me what happened. Give me a story.

a hard life, and now she has died before she got around to the best part. Or at least I hope it would have got better. She died violently. No one deserves that. Before it happened she told us that she had found something important. I hope it was something lasting.

I can't imagine that any sort of belief system can make sense of this. How can you believe in a God or justice or truth when you look at Paula's raped and broken body? Perhaps human life is simply an agony to be born, and our special curse is the attempt to make meaning out of it. Maybe Paula's killer is

remember hearing for the first time. He was old by then, and he had a habit of pulling on the lobe of his ear while talking. He had bad breath; his teeth were slowly rotting in his mouth. We kept our distance, and marvelled at the network of lines carved into his face. As he spoke, his eyebrows rose and fell to make the points. When he told how it happened, it seemed for all the world that he grew younger, and we were back there with him. I can't recall the point of it now, if there was one. Only the story, and the way he told it. I've never been the same since.

He taught them in stories...

no different in value from Paula, just another person who had a need to destroy. But if that's the case, why do I feel so bloody angry? Why do I feel like it's Marilyn and I and everyone who's been violated?

My spiritual explorations seem to have led me up so many blind alleys. If anyone seems to have found a centre, it is Marilyn. But she is reluctant to talk about it, and I'm happy to let her be. I can't help wondering how Paula's death is going to affect us in the long run. It seems a sort of pivot point, but whether for good or for bad it's too early to say.

Meaning Mornay

1 large leavened imagination

Several pinches of salt

3 ample dollops of blarney (good Irish stock is best)

1 bucket of experience

A flexible and generous memory

1 loose tongue (not jellied)

As much wisdom as it is possible to attain
(non-packaged)

Marinate experience in memory for several years—the longer the better.
Make a pocket in the imagination, and fill with the marinated mixture.
Shape into a rough mass, and then roll in a mixture of the salt and wisdom.
Steep in blarney and serve with the tongue.
The finished meal may be assisted with a good red wine (or any red wine).

Paula comes in a dream. She is beautiful. The same Paula, at least recognizable, but very different at the same time. She doesn't say anything. She simply looks at Marilyn, and Marilyn knows that everything is all right. In her hands Paula has a gift. She passes it to Marilyn with a smile. It is clear that it is a gift for some time in the future. Marilyn wants to hold on to Paula, but already she is gone. There is the soul-piercing song of a canary in her wake.

Truth is not a product, to be processed and packaged and dispensed. It is an encounter which takes place when people share their stories in a place of safety and dignity. Anything worth knowing always has a beginning, a middle and an end; and sometimes it takes a while to get from one to the other.

Tell me the old old story...

Before time began, there was God, living in glorious isolation. It had its good points. There were never any arguments about which channel to watch, and nobody asked for the music to be turned down. But it was tedious. No matter how big a miracle God whipped up to relieve the boredom, there

#

It is more than two years now since I last wrote in this journal. We moved flat shortly after Paula's death, and never got around to unpacking everything. I was looking for a screwdriver last night and came across this buried in the bottom of a box. Perhaps it is time to start keeping track again. Marilyn and I are still together. We had a bad patch around six months after the funeral, when Marilyn was severely depressed. She got a job at a job training centre, and that helped.

was no one to applaud. The dinner table was very quiet, and you always knew whose turn it was to do the dishes. So it was that sitting by the fire on a cold night, God began to tell a story. It was a story of a universe and a planet. It started out with water, but God began to throw in things like land and fish and animals. He told it with trees and clouds and mountains and stars.

Eventually, in a sort of climax, he threw in some creatures which he called humans. God became so absorbed in telling this story, he forgot that there was no one to listen. And so it was with some surprise that he began to hear voices. Looking around, he discovered that there was a planet with people on it, and they were calling to him. 'My word,' he exclaimed. 'Where did they come from?'

'What does this mean?' they wanted to know. So, settling back on her haunches, she began to tell them a story...

Our search for truth has borne fruit. I guess we understand now what it was that had happened to Paula before her death, though you can never be sure. Marilyn had what you could only describe as an experience about a year ago. The flow-on effects from that have transformed our lives fairly substantially. Not that we have arrived anywhere, but we feel as if we have at last started out on a journey which is worthwhile. I am unsure exactly where it will lead, but confident about the direction. The world is no less messy than ever it was, but I now have hope.

Is there any truth in the rumour of God? Any sign that there may be meaning in this life: something beyond what is immediately apparent? I can't tell you that. I only have my own experience to go on, and you have yours. But if you have the time, I can tell you a story. And then, when you tell yours, we can listen together and see if we can hear any other voice speaking through them—any hints of the divine. Together, we may have some hope of building a new story.

THE END

#

I am Vincent, of course. I don't know why it is sometimes easier to speak to others in the third person, but there you have it. I've always preferred to tell and listen to stories rather than lectures. What can I tell you? That I love Marilyn and love God, and receive love from both of them. You have your own stories to tell, and mine may make no sense to you. Treat it with tenderness just the same. We are all lost on the face of the earth, swapping our stories to try and find some way ahead.

————————➤ (NOT)

We need each other.

Marilyn came into my life as a gift. We often marvel together as to how it all happened. I hope we will travel together for a long time, perhaps to death. Around her neck she still wears the crucifix.

#

Acknowledgments

We would like to thank all those who have given us permission to include quotations in this book, as indicated in the list below. Every effort has been made to trace and acknowledge copyright holders of all the quotations included in this book. We apologize for any errors or omissions that may remain, and would ask those concerned to contact the publishers, who will ensure that full acknowledgment is made in the future.

Extract from 'Suzanne Takes you Down' taken from *Leonard Cohen Poems 1956–68*, published by Jonathan Cape, 1969.

Extract from 'Sweet Charity' by Cy Colman reprinted by permission of Music Sales Group.

Extract from 'Journey of the Magi' taken from *Collected Poems 1909–62* by T.S. Eliot, published by Faber & Faber Ltd.

'The Road Not Taken' from *Complete Poems of Robert Frost*, ed. Edward Connery Lathem, published by Jonathan Cape. Reprinted by permission of the Estate of Robert Frost.

Extracts from 'Eleanor Rigby' and 'Sgt Pepper's Lonely Hearts Club Band' by Lennon/McCartney reprinted by permission of Music Sales Group.

Extracts from *The Road Less Travelled* by M. Scott Peck reprinted with the permission of Simon & Schuster. Copyright © 1978 by M. Scott Peck MD.

Extracts from 'Do Not Go Gentle into that Good Night' and 'The Force that through the Green Fuse Drives the Flower' taken from *The Poems* by Dylan Thomas, published by J.M. Dent. Reprinted by permission of David Higham Associates.

Also from Lion Publishing

GODZONE
A guide to the travels of the soul

Mike Riddell

In the beginning was the road. The long and winding road that leads... where?

Godzone is a book of mystery and illumination, a guidebook to the travels of the heart. With humour, story-telling and captivating originality it entices the reader to join its hitchhiking author on the most important journey of all...

Mike Riddell has backpacked his own way around the world – earning his passage as (amongst other things) factory-hand, builder's labourer, bank clerk, journalist...

ISBN 0 7459 2413 1

All Lion books are available from
your local bookshop, or can be ordered
direct from Lion Publishing. For a free
catalogue, showing the complete list of
titles available, please contact:

Customer Services Department
Lion Publishing plc
Peter's Way
Sandy Lane West
Oxford OX4 5HG

Tel: (01865) 747550
Fax: (01865) 715152